*Freeing Yourself*

*from the*

*Narcissist*

*in Your Life*

# *Freeing Yourself*

# *from the*

# *Narcissist*

# *in Your Life*

## Linda Martinez-Lewi, Ph.D.

JEREMY P. TARCHER/PENGUIN
*a member of Penguin Group (USA) Inc.*
*New York*

## TARCHER
### PENGUIN

JEREMY P. TARCHER/PENGUIN
Published by the Penguin Group
Penguin Group (USA) Inc., 375 Hudson Street,
New York, New York 10014, USA

USA • Canada • UK • Ireland • Australia
New Zealand • India • South Africa • China

Penguin Books Ltd, Registered Offices: 80 Strand, London WC2R 0RL, England
For more information about the Penguin Group visit penguin.com

First trade paperback edition 2013
Copyright © 2008 by Linda Martinez-Lewi
Most Tarcher/Penguin books are available at special quantity discounts for bulk purchase for sales
promotions, premiums, fund-raising, and educational needs. Special books or book excerpts also can be
created to fit specific needs. For details, write: Special.Markets@us.penguingroup.com.

The Library of Congress catalogued the hardcover edition as follows:

Martinez-Lewi, Linda.
Freeing yourself from the narcissist in your life / Linda Martinez-Lewi.
p.      cm.
Includes bibliographical references and index.
ISBN 978-1-58542-624-9
1. Narcissism.    2. Interpersonal relations.    3. Narcissism—Case studies.
4. Celebrities—Psychology—Case studies.    I. Title.
BF575.N35M37     2008          2007036004
158.2—dc22

ISBN 978-0-39916577-1 (paperback edition)

Printed in the United States of America
5    7    9    10    8    6    4

BOOK DESIGN BY NICOLE LAROCHE

*Por Reymundo Saldaña Martinez*
*Siempre estás en mi corazón.*

*For Peter, my husband, source of perpetual love, intellectual clarity, and creativity*

*For David, my son, giver of compassion and loving-kindness*

*For my family of origin, who taught me the lessons of survival, perseverance, and transformation, sprinkled with life-sustaining humor and music's enduring beauty*

*To the great spiritual masters who inspire us each day to open our hearts and awaken our souls*

# Acknowledgments

I am profoundly grateful to Mitch Horowitz, executive editor at Tarcher/ Penguin, who had a deep understanding of the meaning and spirit of the book from the beginning, and who brought his editorial brilliance to the project with irrepressible enthusiasm. A man of innumerable gifts and talents, Mitch generously guided me along the path with wisdom and an unparalleled respect for the author as an individual.

A very special thank-you to Gabrielle Moss, assistant editor, for her graceful intelligence, her invaluable assistance, and unwavering dedication to producing a worthy book.

Deep gratitude to Paul Lapolla, my agent, mentor, and friend, who guided the process and shaping of the book. Paul served up menus of insightful suggestions and incomparable professional expertise with exquisite tact and kindness and a divine sense of humor.

I am very grateful as well to copy editor Grace McVeigh for her superb, thoughtful work.

# Contents

*Freeing Yourself*

*from the*

*Narcissist*

*in Your Life*

# Preface

Today we feel the powerful reach and dark hold of the high-level narcissist, that vaunted human creature who reconstructs the world to fulfill his omnipotent dreams and grandiose delusions. On life's stage, they are CEOs, national leaders, politicians, movie and television stars, physicians, attorneys, media moguls, high-tech savants. Closer to home they are our spouses, lovers, mothers, fathers, siblings, children, in-laws, bosses, and friends.

In this book, I focus on the high-level narcissist. Standing at the center of his created universe, the narcissist, a master image maker, perpetuates an illusion of perfection and power. He exudes an intoxicating charm. Famous high-level narcissists are particularly intriguing. Dramatizing and vivifying this unique personality disorder are scenes from the lives of Pablo Picasso—*"Yo Rey,"* I, the King; Armand Hammer—Ruthless Manipulator; Ayn Rand—Self-Obsessed Virtuoso; and Frank Lloyd Wright—Mother's Perfect Creation.

The high-level narcissist marches through his many geographies, conquering new territories, multiplying his limitless control of the outside world and the lives of those who touch his. Excited followers anticipate his mood and moves, praying for a favorable word or glance. The chosen dwell within his *cercle d'or*, chanting hosannas to his greatness. While his audience is dazzled, the super-narcissist assesses each subject's worth to *him*. He plays upon their proclivities and weaknesses. Despite the years you have known him, the hard work you have done, the love that you express, the sacrifices you have made, the intimacies you believe you shared—eventually the narcissist will cut you off at the knees, even attempt to destroy you if he perceives you as an obstacle to his feverish drive toward ultimate power, control, and omnipotence.

The narcissistic personality is a deeply ingrained, fixed personality structure that most likely will never change. Certainly, high-level narcissists will not be offering themselves as candidates for therapy. They are preoccupied with climbing the power ladder, threatening competitors, enhancing their professional and personal image, and making lots of money.

The gift of the high-level narcissist is an engraved invitation for you to become more authentic, to stretch your psychological muscles, and to seek spiritual awareness. Beyond narcissism, removed from the fray of embattled egos, the noisy hum of greed, the cravings to "always have more," to "win" at all costs, we find peace in a reality without delusion. Life absent insight is a gaudy picture show, a tiresome charade. Within this new reality, we are driven to seek the truth, to peel off the masks of false selves, and to embrace the creative loving force ever present at the center of our being.

# PART ONE

## The Great

## Performer

# CHAPTER ONE

# At Center Stage:

# Outshining All the Others

*He was like a cock who thought the sun had risen to hear him crow.*

— GEORGE ELIOT, ADAM BEDE[1]

*We had a lot in common. I loved him and he loved him.*

— SHELLEY WINTERS[2]

We never know when or under what circumstances we will meet a narcissist. By accident or design we will eventually encounter him. We are often woefully unprepared for these events. I recall an evening, a business/social affair, hosted by a West Coast power couple. The location—a sprawling estate in an exclusive beach enclave of southern California. The mansion was the frequent setting for illustrious fêtes, political gatherings, and elegant soirées. I was invited as a former business consultant to the couple. Other party guests included a private pilot, a plastic surgeon, a superior court judge, a film director, and various sycophants and court jesters, all chartered members of the couple's inner circle.

Greg and Charlene, the decorous hosts, greeted me at the grand entryway. The house was sumptuous in every detail, mimicking the architectural lines of an elaborate wedding cake. Inside, all was elegant and pristine: precious antiques, sterling silver sets, flawless interior design, fragrant white orchids floating in Baccarat vases, the finest bone china, prized contemporary paintings and sculptures. Early in the evening Charlene, the wife and co-owner of the business empire, introduced herself to me, settling into the couch where I sat. From that moment on she never stopped talking about herself—her business triumphs, her material acquisitions, her innumerable trips and treks, her social A-list friends, her couturier, her brilliant and talented children.

During hot and cold hors d'oeuvres, which included stuffed grape leaves from the vineyard on the premises, guests were taken on a prolonged tour of Greg's wine cellar, a commodious series of rooms set at perfect temperatures to protect his priceless collection. Dinner was announced and guests were escorted to a high-ceilinged dining room with walls of dark wood. As I entered, my gaze traveled up the four walls of the room. Many eyes looked out at me, the innocent faces of large wild animals felled—hunting trophies: antelope, deer, elk, buffalo. Surely the owners of this house had used the skills of the finest taxidermist to achieve the riveting effect. I had to keep myself from darting out of the room. I felt nauseated and wondered how it was possible for people to ingest food in the presence of these dead creatures who had been affixed to the walls in a perverse kind of crucifixion.

During dinner Charlene made a deliberate point of telling everyone in earshot that their estate was on a special annual home tour. She described in detail all the reconstruction they had conducted after purchasing the mansion. The repainting of the home had taken more than three years, and Charlene was still not satisfied. She had a master painter on call in case they decided to make quick changes. Ancient marble imported from Italian quarries held a prominent presence throughout the house, giving it the atmosphere of a mausoleum.

After dinner Charlene continued her breathless litany of self, signaling a chilling disdain for others who would never measure up to her standards. Everything surrounding Charlene and her golden circle was perfect. Outside this boundary were inferior, pitiful beings, condemned to a dull hell of mediocrity. Inside this hallowed sphere were the privileged, who surrounded and protected her like a venerated member of royalty. When the interminable evening ended and I said my good-byes, I felt like a long-held prisoner now freed. As I raced across the magnificent green lawn, I gratefully embraced the clear star-filled night and realized that in all those hours she had not *once* asked me one question about myself.

This book focuses on the high-level narcissist, masters of charm, purveyors of magnetism. Meeting one of these individuals is a memorable experience whether the encounter is positive, negative, or mixed. Narcissists beguile and persuade with a special brand of magic.

My purpose is to inform the reader so that he will be able to identify the narcissistic personality and, in particular, the high-level narcissists in his life and to develop a full appreciation that these individuals suffer from a severe personality disorder. Being unaware and uninformed of the psychopathology, origins, and unconscious motivations of the narcissistic personality disorder is counterproductive and injurious to those who naively tangle with narcissists. Arming yourself with specific strategic tools offered in this book provides you with the psychological edge and confidence you will bring to all of your encounters with the high-level narcissist.

In Part I, The Great Performer, we view the narcissist at center stage, the spotlight shining fully on him. This is dramatically illustrated in vivid scenes from the life of art world icon Pablo Picasso, who epitomizes the high-level narcissist in full bloom. To clarify the diagnostic distinctions between the narcissist and other personality disorders, I draw the differences between him and the borderline personality disorder and the antisocial personality. I present a historical and societal perspective, explaining how the dramatic shift in psychopathology has changed from a focus on the neuroses to a focus on the personality disorders.

Today, society encourages the ascendance of high-level narcissists, rewarding them with extraordinary financial success, social status, public and private adulation. Narcissists pervade every realm of life today. They are our CEOs, actors, politicians, world leaders, physicians, attorneys, judges, entrepreneurs. The high-level narcissist spins grandiose delusions that feed his feelings of superiority and overriding self-entitlement. When I refer to the high-level narcissist as he, I am including female narcissists as well.

More recently, the world courts high-level narcissists; they are highly prized and envied, frequently treated like royalty. The narcissist's interactions with others are shallow and venal. He keeps people in his circle as long as they benefit him. When they become an inconvenience or cost him money he is unwilling to spend on some unrealistic venture he has contrived, or become rivals, they are dismissed without warning, gone as if they never existed. Despite this craven ruthlessness, the narcissist believes that he is an honorable human being. Blinded by his smooth charm and contagious dynamism, his golden circle of followers and sycophants applaud and cater to his smallest wish and whim.

The high-level narcissist makes no distinction between image and self. Incapable of dealing with his inner world of hurt, mistakes, cruelties, traumas, self-delusions, he fabricates an impeccable self-image. The high-level narcissist chooses those who will loyally serve him, even sacrifice themselves for him. Often they are physically attractive, talented, and bright or present a combination of these qualities. The narcissist feels expansive and activated encircled by this crew of faithful devotees. His horizons are limitless; the meticulously honed image of self has become a living reality.

In Part II, Behind the Perfect Mask, I describe through clinical vignettes and anecdotes the hidden inner personality traits of the narcissist. My purpose is to familiarize you, the reader, with the tools to identify the high-level narcissists in your life and to understand that you are confronting a severe personality disorder not a benign character eccentricity. Here we encounter the dark underworld of his psyche. The high-level narcissist is an exploiter par excellence. I have painfully observed how he has skillfully manipulated, seduced, and burned the same individuals more than once. This attests to his gifts of cunning and persuasion. Not having a conscience is a plus for him. There is always a core group surrounding the high-level narcissist who will never leave him no matter what the cost to their own lives.

The high-level narcissist appears to have a deception gene. You can make a deal with a narcissist, legalize it, and discover that he suddenly has changed his mind and will not honor his commitment. Once he makes a decision to change course, the curtain falls abruptly, offices are closed, borrowed money is left unpaid. Deception becomes an art form in the hands of a high-level narcissist. Automatic lies and obfuscations are all part of his permanent repertoire. A portrait of the ignominious industrialist and "philan-thropist" Armand Hammer demonstrates the ruthless manipula-tions and treacheries he perpetrated to achieve his delusional visions of glory.

The high-level narcissist often spends his childhood years and beyond as the golden child, the one chosen above the rest. Usually, one parent takes the lead, deciding that a particular child who is beautiful, handsome, talented, or athletic will carry this role. He or she represents the fulfillment of a parental need. The mother and/or father *live through* this child to respond to *their* early psychologi-cal deprivations.

The life of Frank Lloyd Wright, the great American architect, is a perfect example of this pathological pattern. An unbroken golden thread joined Wright to his mother most of his life. From his earliest years, Wright's mother, Anna, communicated to him in words and deeds that her son was a god, that he would become the world's greatest architect and could do no wrong. Always ambiva-lent about her cloying and controlling manner, Wright remained emotionally fused with Anna most of his life.

The parents of high-level narcissists are often narcissistic themselves. Their children suffer from a "cold embrace," the pre-tense of authentic caring. The self-absorbed narcissistic parent di-rects the show, turning his child into an acquiescent puppet. This parent blocks his child's right to become a solid separate individ-ual. Narcissistic personality disorders develop a false grandiose self rather than an authentic true self.

Beneath the bravado and grandiosity lies a pervasive empti-ness. The high-level narcissist constantly turns to the rewards of the external world (praise, adulation, material possessions) to fill the painful inner void. The narcissist projects a bottomless rage, secret envy, and closet paranoia. The narcissistic ego is brittle, vulnerable to perceived psychological injuries and slights. In later years the high-level narcissist is often crushed by a sinking enervating despair.

The narcissist suffers from a hardened heart, and is incapable of empathy. Lack of empathy is a signature personality trait for diagnosing the narcissistic personality disorder. The high-level narcissist activates a finely honed pseudo-empathy, which is persuasive with most individuals.

I focus on the life of famous philosopher and novelist, Ayn Rand, as an example of a high-level narcissist who led a self-obsessed life devoid of empathy. Ayn Rand ruthlessly and with exquisite calculation decided what she wanted and whom she wanted. She would not be deterred in the arena of spreading her philosophy of Objectivism or in satisfying her erotic and sexual passions. From beginning to end, she led a life of the hardened heart, in that cold darkness where the warmth of empathy cannot take root.

True empathy begins at the core, the heart. Here, I introduce the idea that the ancient Indian practice of hatha yoga can free up blocked energies in our bodies and minds. The use of proper breathing techniques and a series of body postures facilitates health, expands the heart center, activating a sense of peace and vitality. Another source for developing empathy is through consciously dealing with the truth of our own suffering.

Following a spiritual path nurtures our empathic qualities. Those who persevere discover greater transparency in themselves and a deeper love for others.

In Part III, The Adoring Audience, I describe the golden circle of followers and devotees that the high-level narcissist creates. Inside the circle is a sacred space reserved for handpicked members who believe that the narcissist is the source from which their identities and feelings of worth flow.

A classic case of mentor worship is described in the relationship between architectural genius Frank Lloyd Wright and his elaborate circles of admirers. In his tempestuous personal life Wright had several wives and a mistress. His last wife, Olgivanna, sacrificed herself to perpetuate Wright's greatness, inviting the world to worship him as a god.

Some high-level narcissists have accumulated, earned, or inherited great wealth. Many of them use money and its privileges as perfect bait to draw the chosen to their inner circle. Wealth is the balm and lure that attracts and holds prospective and long-term members of this elite group. The ugly side of this cozy equation is revealed in the sacrifice of self, and the abuse and humiliations that many members endure in exchange for their privileged status.

Many of those who live with or work for a high-level narcissist recognize that they are leading their lives through someone else. They have squelched their creativity, drive, and identities for a tyrant. They are counterfeits with pleasing ways designed to keep their master narcissistically fulfilled. When the final blows are struck and the curtain of disillusionment has fallen, some exhausted and distraught followers switch roles from adoring believers to intimate enemies.

In Part IV, Response to the Great Performer, I offer specific rules of engagement that will maximize all of your interactions with the high-level narcissist. The source of your success is keen awareness of your *own* core psychological issues. Feeling secure within yourself and psychologically grounded is essential. Stay mindful in the present moment with the issue at hand. Honor your moral and ethical values. There are rules for dealing with the boss and the boardroom. Outfox the high-level narcissist by taking the initiative, defending yourself without being defensive, and always have plans B, C, and D ready for execution.

In the last chapter, "Beyond Narcissism," I invite the reader to travel to another land, to a quiet spaciousness that puts life in a clearer, simpler perspective. We will build a bridge together that will transport you beyond the ego-driven frenzy of the narcissistic world. Here you can learn how to become more still and peaceful inside. One method is the practice of meditation. I offer specific suggestions for starting a meditation practice.

Those who open this door are encouraged to drop their egos, remove false masks, and live authentically. Beyond narcissism there are no boundaries. Knowing this, we experience ourselves as unique living fragments of an evolving, dynamic, beatific whole.

In numerous conversations when I describe the character traits of a high-level narcissist with friends and acquaintances, I frequently hear: "Oh my God, that was my former boyfriend. The best thing I ever did was leave that egotistical, deceitful bastard" or "That's my lying, demanding ex-wife to a tee" or "You just described my mother-in-law, a self-absorbed perfectionist; nothing's ever good enough for her" or "That two-faced scum; everyone thought he walked on water. During our entire marriage he never missed an opportunity to have an affair, a fling, or a one-night stand. When I finally became ill and couldn't tolerate it anymore, I asked him for a divorce. I picked the wrong lawyers and got completely screwed financially. I can only be grateful that this horrible man is out of my life."

To survive and flourish, we all need healthy narcissism. This is a positive feeling of self-worth. A person with healthy narcissism has a firm realistic sense of self. By respecting and caring for ourselves, we acknowledge that we are unique and valuable human beings. We can love others only if we possess healthy self-love. Having compassion for ourselves, we learn to forgive our mistakes, big and small. When we falter and fail as imperfect beings, healthy narcissism allows us to acknowledge our waywardness without defensiveness and to make necessary changes in our behavior and attitudes. It carries us along with a sense of hope and optimism. Those who have a quality of balanced self-love also possess a spontaneous bedrock of humor that is simultaneously capable of viewing both the unadorned truth and the comic absurdity of life.

It should be noted that many high achievers are *not* narcissistic personalities. They are bright, motivated, and talented—driven to be their best. They are capable of love and intimacy with spouses, partners, children, relatives, and friends. They possess a self-effacing manner despite their worldly achievements and the exalted opinions of others. They know and accept that they are imperfect human beings. Alongside their talents and many accomplishments, these individuals display warmth, conscience, and kindness.

Unhealthy or pathological narcissism moves along a different track. The narcissist is deceptive and manipulative in *all* of his relationships. The sine qua non of pathological narcissism is an obsessive self-absorption combined with the inability to experience genuine empathy toward others. The word *narcissism* originates from the myth of Narcissus. In this ancient story the nymph Echo falls in love with the beautiful youth Narcissus. Becoming very angry when Narcissus does not return her love, Echo asks Aphrodite, the goddess of love, to take revenge by making Narcissus the victim of unrequited love. One day while walking through the forest, Narcissus kneels beside a spring to drink. As he gazes into the clear waters, he sees a youth so handsome that he falls hopelessly in love with him. He becomes so obsessed with this apparition that he can neither eat nor drink. He dies of starvation, never realizing that the nymph he sought was his own reflection in the water.

Picasso—the enunciation of his name evokes primal images of the man and his art. The two are inseparable from each other. Whether manically working in his studio on his latest painting motif (often of women with whom he was beginning, having, or ending affairs), on vacation *en famille* with a mistress nearby, or at the bullfights posing in white, riveted to the ancient bloody spectacle, Picasso always stole the show. He controlled the life scripts of his players—wives, mistresses, girlfriends, children, business associates, enemies—as facilely and deliberately as he created his paintings, drawings, etchings, and ceramics. When Picasso was present, the sun was out and the crowd gathered. It was carnival, fiesta—an endless raucous party. Along with the light of his talent, Picasso harvested a violent unrelenting darkness upon others in the form of stabbing emotional abandonment, chronic deception, sexual sadism, psychological coldness, and steely revenge.

Pablo's greatest artistic masterpiece was in "being Picasso." Even at the age of eighteen this famous narcissist was already openly expressing his inflated sense of self-importance. Before leaving his parents and friends for Paris to realize his dreams of artistic greatness, Picasso displayed a self-portrait "with the inscription *Yo Rey*—'I the King.' "[3] It was one incident in a multitude of scenes from Picasso's life in which he extolled his belief in his superior, demigod nature.

Pablo was notorious for collecting mistresses and lovers, as if harvesting fragrant, exotic flowers for a celebratory bouquet. In his ninety-one years Picasso produced tens of thousands of works of art, two wives, four children, numerous lovers and mistresses.

Françoise Gilot, a gifted art student, likely played his most favored mistress, muse, and companion in art.

Françoise grew up with a father who was difficult, demanding, and very disappointed that she had not been born a son. He made her perform physical feats that scared her—climbing up and down hills, swimming tremendous distances with greater and greater speed. Françoise substituted her extreme fear for anger and resentment. Françoise learned to love the seduction of danger, and this included her decision to share her life with Picasso. It was both a challenge and a dangerous thrill. Françoise met the master when she was twenty-one and he was sixty-one. Young, naive, and seduced by his talent and sheer dynamic force, Françoise began to meet with Picasso, although he was still married to (but separated from) Olga Khokhlova, his first wife, a former ballerina. Olga had become a pariah to Picasso with her obsessional rantings and constant spying on her estranged husband and his newest lover. After they had lived apart for a while, Françoise could no longer resist Picasso. She moved in with him, and eventually they had two children, Claude and Paloma. In her intimate and revealing biography, *Life with Picasso*, Françoise quotes his deprecatory words toward women: "For me there are only two kinds of women—goddesses and doormats."[4] Gilot replies: "And whenever he thought I might be feeling too much like a goddess, he did his best to turn me into a doormat."[5]

In his personal relationships with women, Picasso insisted that he alone was the central current of their desire. He reveled in orchestrating cruel and psychologically pernicious scenarios in which women would vie for his attention and actually fight over him. On one occasion, Picasso instigated and witnessed a physical fight between his voracious young lover Marie-Thérèse Walter and Dora Maar, a current girlfriend and intimate. Like any classic narcissist, Picasso was able to dispose of women who no longer served him. Pablo arrived at a solution for dealing with past wives: "Every time I change wives I should burn the last one. . . . They wouldn't be around now to complicate my existence."[6]

With Picasso, those closest to him in particular had to be well trained and ever ready for combat. He loved to create snares and traps that made others feel small and inadequate. Gilot points out that to gain Picasso's respect, you had to play the part of worthy opponent "because life for Pablo was always a game one played with no holds barred."[7] Watching the many people that Picasso tricked and humiliated, Françoise survived his ruses: "And so I learned very early that no matter how fond you might be of Pablo, the only way to keep his respect was to be prepared for the worst and take action before he did."[8]

During complex liaisons and emotionally damaging, sadistic games, Picasso would tell each of the women that he wanted to be exclusively with her and then turn around and repeat the same lie to the other partner. Simultaneously, he painted each woman in a motif and style that depicted whether she was rising or falling from his sexual and romantic ardor. Layers of intrigue and cruelty against women were devised by Picasso to inflict pain and to demonstrate his absolute control over them, much like the haughty pirouettes of a matador during a triumphant pass with a bleeding bull.

With all of her devotion to Pablo's art and his life and their children, Françoise finally recognized that this master artist was incapable of true empathy and tenderness: "and then gradually [I] came to realize that human warmth was something I would never get from Pablo."[9] When Françoise gave clear indications that her separation from Picasso was becoming imminent, he derided her, saying that she would never be recognized or appreciated as an individual but always be seen solely as a person attached to a great and talented man. He fueled the tirade: "Even if you think people like you, it will only be a kind of curiosity they will have about a person whose life has touched mine so intimately. . . . For you, reality is finished. . . . If you attempt to take a step outside my reality—you're headed straight for the desert."[10]

Picasso was not finished. He devised an exquisite signature revenge for Françoise. He convinced her that the two of them were destined to get back together. He insisted that Françoise obtain a divorce from her husband, Luc Simon, promising marriage and the legitimization of Claude and Paloma. Françoise proceeded, believing that she would be reunited with Pablo. Françoise obtained the divorce. She waited. One morning while reading a newspaper, she discovered that Pablo had precipitously married Jacqueline Roque. The shock and betrayal of this ignominious act was crippling, but Françoise survived. In the end the woman triumphantly still standing was Françoise Gilot. It was *she* who had severed the relationship with the master. And it was *she* who moved forward as an artist and an independent woman.

Marina Picasso, Picasso's granddaughter, speaks frankly of the profound effects of her grandfather's cruelty and negligence on her personally. Everyone else's life had to stop in midair—their activities, feelings, thoughts, words—on the oscillating winds of Picasso's moods, whims, vanities, passions, impulsivities, and perversities of the moment. Each one of Marina's closest family members was left broken, crushed, or eventually destroyed by this man. Marina observes: "No one in my family ever managed to escape from the stranglehold of this genius."[11] Her father, Paulo (Picasso's son), a chronic alcoholic, spent his days haplessly begging Picasso for sustenance to keep food on his family's table. He was a lifelong captive of his father's predictable inflictions of shame and degradation. In every way, spoken and unspoken, Picasso never missed an opportunity to let his son know just what a worthless failure he was and would always be. Unable to separate himself psychologically from Picasso and activate his individuality, Paulo remained tied to his father like an infant sucking on a cold mother's milkless teat. In the end, Paulo drowned in the alcohol that he had used so long to remove himself from the pain of not being loved. The sweet but deadly oblivion that he sought finally consumed him.

The brilliant Picasso sun at the center burned others in exquisite ways. His former wife and ballerina, Olga, counted her days as an emotional and physical invalid, desperately searching the past for happier times when she was Picasso's woman. Emilienne, Picasso's daughter-in-law and reluctant mother to Marina and Pablito, infused her imagination with blatant fantasies of Picasso's desire to seduce her. Every in and out breath was attached to Picasso. Emilienne, the promiscuous adolescent mother, was incapable of providing any semblance of protection and care for her children. Pablito (Marina's brother), lost and unloved by father, mother, and grandfather, clung to Marina as long as he could. Finally, he took his short life by drinking bleach, bleeding himself out. Marina, the survivor, spent much of her life unsuccessfully seeking her grandfather's love and approval. The childhood image is that of an urchin clutching her brother Pablito's hand as they stand at the elaborate heavy gates of Picasso's latest castle. The face is prematurely knowing and forlorn. Even at the tenderest age, Marina understood she was not welcome. Marina triumphed over what she calls the Picasso virus to become a humanitarian to starving and needy orphans.[12]

Narcissistic individuals are often very successful and innovative in their professional lives. This was the case with Pablo Picasso. Combining God-given talent and enormous drive, Picasso transformed the face of modern art. In his personal life he exploited and abused the women around him and abandoned his children.

Ultimately, it was the power he achieved and the adulation of the world, which he craved, that mattered to him as much as his need to create. Near the end of his life, Picasso produced a self-portrait that tells us everything about this narcissistically vengeful man. In this painting, the artist has ripped off his final mask. "It was the face of frozen anguish and primordial horror. . . . It was the horror he had painted and the anguish he had caused and which, in his own anguish, he continued to cause."[13] Beneath the adoration, fame, and talent, one beholds the distorted wretched face of a desperate madman.

## MAKING DISTINCTIONS

In this book I focus on the high-level narcissist, the omnipotent, grandiose, often charismatic individual of overreaching ambition and palpable hubris. He games at life rather than living it. The height and breadth of his stack of poker chips and the lush green of his winnings are all that matter. Showing disingenuous compassion or concern for others is a clever stage act the high-level narcissist uses to convince others to play his game. Most people are fooled or seduced by the narcissist's heady promises. Often financially very successful with the privileges of material largesse, the narcissist becomes an object of desire for those who live in simpler, duller circumstances. Many individuals are so impressed with the financial and social status of a narcissist that they become willing worshipers. Whether you are sleeping with him, working for him, or believe you are a member of his inner circle, the sole purpose of his relationship with you is always about his winning and the rewards that flow from you to *him alone.*

The *Diagnostic and Statistical Manual of Mental Disorders* (*DSM-IV-TR*), published by the American Psychiatric Association, is a professional guide used by clinicians for diagnosing a wide variety of mental disorders. It is a comprehensive diagnostic tool with certain limitations. The *DSM-IV-TR* is descriptive in nature. Diagnoses are based heavily on listing specific symptoms and pathological behaviors rather than focusing on psychodynamic unconscious pathological issues associated with the full spectrum of life beginning in early childhood. It does not address the inner psychic core of these individuals.

The *DSM-IV-TR* outlines character traits and behaviors for diagnosing an individual as a narcissistic personality disorder:[14]

A pervasive pattern of grandiosity (in fantasy or behavior), need for admiration, and lack of empathy, beginning by early adulthood and present in a variety of contexts, as indicated by five (or more) of the following:

1. has a grandiose sense of self-importance (e.g., exaggerates achievements and talents, expects to be recognized as superior without commensurate achievements)

2. is preoccupied with fantasies of unlimited success, power, brilliance, beauty, or ideal love

3. believes that he or she is "special" and unique and can only be understood by, or should associate with, other special or high-status people (or institutions)

4. requires excessive admiration

5. has a sense of entitlement—i.e., unreasonable expectations of especially favorable treatment or automatic compliance with his or her expectations

6. is interpersonally exploitative, i.e., takes advantage of others to achieve his or her own ends

7. lacks empathy: is unwilling to recognize or identify with the feelings and needs of others

8. is often envious of others or believes that others are envious of him or her

9. shows arrogant, haughty behaviors or attitudes

Narcissists are complex human beings. They come in all flavors and sizes. They are male and female, young and old, wealthy and poor, smart and not so bright, educated and uneducated, sophisticated and unworldly. Although they are defined by distinct personality traits, there are gradations and shades among them. Like the subtlest differences in a palette of color or range of notes on a scale, each narcissist is sui generis.

There are high- and low-level narcissists, and layers in between. The low-level narcissist has a personality constellation similar to his more "successful" brother, but his diminished level of functioning in a career and social relationships is striking. He has difficulty driving himself to reach the higher peaks of achievement. He suffers a deficit of the steely confidence of a supernarcissist. He is afraid of taking risks that are crucial for landing the big fish. Absent the charm and charisma so palpable in the high-level narcissist, he is much less talented at seducing and manipulating others. The low-level narcissist suffers from chronic depression that breaks through his imperfect defenses.

Todd, an assistant film director, never feels at ease. He is always secretly afraid that a more aggressive player will come along and usurp the power that he has struggled to gain. Those who work for Todd dread his presence. He is known for making unrealistic demands on his colleagues and employees. Unwilling to compromise, he often gets into nasty disputes with his bosses, insisting that the right answers and solutions to problems reside with him alone. These rigid personality traits continually abort his professional climb. He loses prospective jobs. With each failure, Todd experiences dark moods that become debilitating. He drinks to excess to dissipate hidden feelings of failure. Todd appears to recover enough to pursue another project. In his personal life Todd is secretive and deceptive. Todd chooses partners who are needy and masochistic. Incapable of true intimacy, he uses women to make himself feel sexually potent and psychologically dominant. When they finally grow tired of his constant demeaning attacks, Todd eagerly replaces them with a new face and body. Todd stumbles through life falling short—believing that he is superior but never obtaining the heady goals he knows he deserves. Todd can be described as a low-level narcissistic personality.

Some self-obsessed, indulgent individuals appear to be narcissistic. Their constant self-referential statements and need for attention and applause can lead you to believe this is the case. Observing them more carefully, we notice that they are capable of empathy and warmth. They have the ability to give, to understand, and to reach out when someone is in pain or need. The self-absorption and demands for attention so prevalent in their behaviors are unconscious defenses they use to ward off buried feelings of worthlessness and deprivation. They may be neurotic, histrionic, or a combination of different disorders, but they are not narcissistic personalities.

The borderline personality suffers from a profound fear of abandonment. He tends to develop intense interpersonal relationships that contain highly charged emotionality. He may desperately fuse with an intimate one moment and, in the next, turn aggressively hostile. Borderlines are terrified of being alone and constantly feel a sense of impending psychological annihilation. Inside, they experience a pervasive feeling of intolerable emptiness. Impulsive and susceptible to rapid mood shifts, they are known for swift forays into sexual- and substance-abuse acting-out behaviors. Their feelings of incessant desperation are often demonstrated in dramatic suicidal gestures. Beneath their extraordinary personal ordeals, the borderline can empathize deeply with the psychological pain of others.

Narcissists are incapable of empathy. When they extend themselves, it is all part of an elaborate act that enhances their image as a "good person." The defenses of the borderline are tenuous at best, exposing deep fissures of vulnerability to the slightest changes in their environment. Unlike the narcissist who defends himself with a strong sense of entitlement and superiority, the borderline never feels that life is going smoothly. He is continually in a state of flux, with the sands always shifting beneath his imperiled feet.

In making a distinction between the narcissist and the antisocial personality (psychopathic, sociopathic, dyssocial personality disorder), it is essential to note that the major clinical feature of the antisocial personality, according to the *DSM-IV-TR*, is "a pervasive pattern of disregard for, and violation of, the rights of others that begins in childhood or early adolescence and continues into adulthood."[15] These individuals often have a history of conduct disorder.[16] This psychological disturbance is diagnosed before the age of eighteen. It is defined by aggressive and harmful behavior to humans and animals. They are often bullies who are physically violent and use various weapons to harm others. They engage in theft, breaking into homes, places of business, and cars. They often con people out of money and property. When they commit crimes and transgress societal laws and mores, they feel no sense of guilt or remorse.

The antisocial personality consistently commits in unlawful acts, refuses to obey society's laws, and flagrantly behaves in destructive patterns that frequently require arrest and punishment. It is not unusual for them to destroy the personal property of others and to be involved in illegal professions. They wantonly jeopardize the safety of others. They neglect their children and other members of their family, treating them with indifference and abuse. They view their victims as stupid or foolish. The antisocial personality lies in a malevolent way. Not only is he unempathic, he holds a cold contempt for others. He is aggressive and recklessly impulsive, endangering his own life and those who surround him. Unlike the narcissist who is obsessed with his image, the antisocial personality places little value on his public persona or whether he is held in esteem or damnation.[17]

Jesse was so handsome as a little boy that he could be described as beautiful. Perfectly formed, with delicately sculpted features, he looked as if he belonged in a full-page color layout in a slick fashion magazine. At age three, Jesse was cocky. He knew he was adorable and good-looking. No one ever said no to him. His father, Spence, was often out of town, "doing deals." Jesse grew up being told by Spence that the name of the game was survival and that the law was there to be circumvented not obeyed. The boy learned early that it was always best to make quick, easy money. Adhering to laws was inconvenient and slow; they were made to be broken. His mother, Felicia, worshiped her son and set no limits. She dismissed his repeated cruelties to playmates and his coarse rudeness with adults. Jesse learned to steal early. He pilfered candy and small items at first, distracting clerks with his twinkling cobalt-blue eyes. In his teens he broke into houses with a school friend, taking valuables with the deftness and casual attitude of a hardened criminal. Often truant, he used his gifts of persuasion with teachers to maintain passing grades. Felicia idolized her son and continued to make excuses for him when he broke the law or injured others. He was a masculine idol with young women. He fathered several children, whom he abandoned without a wisp of conscience. On several occasions, he forced himself physically on unwilling female partners. He intimidated his victims by threatening bodily harm if they spoke up. He called these incidents "fooling around," not rape.

In his early twenties, Jesse, now a full-blown antisocial personality, graduated to sophisticated white-collar crimes that involved trapping naive affluent people into high-risk investment funds that were bogus and unlawful. By the time the unwitting investors discovered that their savings had been drained, Jesse and his criminal partners had vanished. Armed with new identities, they plotted and designed sticky new webs for fresh victims.

## A PSYCHODYNAMIC APPROACH TO
## THE NARCISSISTIC PERSONALITY

In this book I take a psychodynamic approach to analyzing the taproots of the narcissistic personality. By "psychodynamic" I mean the complex interplay between conscious and unconscious emotional and mental processes that create and sustain the individual personality. A foremost contemporary school of psychoanalytic theory, which includes extensive research and therapeutic application, is called object relations. The word *object* means "other" (mother, father, surrogate parental figure). "Object relations" refers to the earliest relationships of infants and young children with their parent(s). From birth the full range of interactions between parent and child and the spectrum of emotions attached to them are internalized into the child's developing psyche. Emotions communicated between mother (or surrogate parents) are both pleasurable and frustrating. The great psychoanalyst Otto Kernberg, explains it this way: "More specifically, from birth on, our relations with significant others, under the impact of strong affects (emotions), are internalized as affective memory. These basic affective memories contain the representation of the self, the representation of [the] other—called 'object' in object relations theory—and the dominant affect linking them."[18]

## FROM NEUROSIS TO NARCISSISM

In the last fifty years there has been a dramatic shift, a sea change, in the occurrence and recognition of psychological disturbances from neuroses to personality disorders, which include narcissism. Freud treated patients who suffered from hysterical symptoms (physical symptoms with psychological origins), neuroses, and obsessive-compulsive disorders. In the thirties and forties neurotic maladies were prevalent. Today, psychoanalysts, psychiatrists, and psychotherapists are seeing a plethora of patients who suffer from disturbances of the self. Prominent among these are borderline conditions and narcissistic disorders, pathological constellations rooted at the very core of the personality.

Most narcissistic personalities never seek psychological treatment. They are comfortable with themselves, feeling no need to change. When others around them are suffering from his horrendous conduct, the narcissist scratches his head with insouciance and wonders why there's such a fuss. Narcissists blame their intimates, labeling them demanding, spoiled, dependent, and mentally unstable. Why should a narcissist endure the painful hours of humiliation, self-doubt, the reliving of traumas connected with the therapeutic process. Why would he want to level with himself and come clean. Why should he acknowledge and take responsibility for the pain he has caused others. Why would he expose his weaknesses to a probing professional. The narcissist belongs to a different psychological faith, whose first commandment is to never prostrate oneself on the altar of truth.

Present-day society reinforces the narcissist's inflated self-image by handsomely rewarding him with worldly power, enormous salaries, and perks. Some professions naturally attract narcissists. Two fields in particular—entertainment and politics—provide endless opportunities for narcissists to activate and be rewarded for their unique personality traits. Of course, not all individuals in these professions are narcissistic. Being the object of adulation as a result of appearing in a movie or on a television screen is the ultimate fantasy for many narcissists. What can be headier than to have one's visual image flashed across the world.

Currently, the line between actor and politician has blurred. Like actors preparing for a part, politicians hire professional speechwriters, coaches, spin masters, and handlers to guarantee that they will deliver "the message" that elects them to office.

Today's politicians are obsessed with image—razor-cut hair, custom toupees, firm chin and jaw lines, expertly coordinated wardrobes. Gestures, body moves, folksy stories, even certain kinds of smiles are scripted. Winning mantras and gag lines are practiced religiously. Candidates crowd the TV cameras, excitedly waiting to deliver their best sound bite of the day. On television, in movies, and in magazines we are assailed by the external image. Physical attractiveness has become an essential ingredient of success. Beauty and handsomeness are equated with winning and monetary achievements. The deification of self has emerged as a dawning New Age religion. The constant pressure to achieve a perfect face and body are symptomatic of this era of narcissism. Aesthetic imperfections—cottage-cheese thighs; asymmetrical, small, or sagging breasts; large noses; wrinkles or age spots—have become a subject of ridicule that produces intense shame among women in particular (even those in their twenties and thirties). Visual signs of aging are feared and detested. Grandma and Grandpa are hidden and often warehoused in old-age homes long before their time. They are an embarrassment in a society that worships externals: flat stomachs; unwrinkled, taut flawless skin; razor-sharp jowlless chin lines; perfectly matched breasts; full lips; pumped muscles; invisible veins; hairless ears and nostrils; luxurious thick manes of hair. In this culture no one dies—they get a face-lift. Women, horrified by gaining weight, are trapped in dangerous cycles of starvation, bingeing, and purging. Repulsed by the slightest weight gain, they punish themselves with strenuous exercise and voluntary starvation that perpetuate self-hatred in secret. The pursuit of the perfect image has supplanted the quest for something quieter, less visible, and more meaningful—personal integrity and truthfulness.

Today we are surrounded by narcissists. On the illuminated stage of life they are movie and television stars, CEOs, politicians, attorneys, physicians, business moguls. Closer to home, they are our spouses, ex-spouses, lovers, partners, parents, in-laws, siblings, and friends. Facing down the narcissist eye-to-eye, while remaining psychologically grounded and true to ourselves, is a daunting task.

The houselights go down, audience whispers cease, the curtain goes up—the spotlight shines on the actor at stage center—the show begins. This is the metaphor for the narcissistic personality. He always plays the starring role, performing brilliantly with believability and flourish. He has rehearsed his lines all of his life: every word, nuance, tone. This is his magic moment. He becomes energized, electrified as he basks in the glory of the full attention of the audience. If the focus wavers away from him even for a moment, he skillfully brings it back to himself. With the spotlight on him once more, he is fully recharged as he deeply inhales all the adulation and praise, the psychological air that he breathes.

It is ten P.M. The crew started at six A.M. They have been working sixteen-hour days, seven days a week for over a month. Darryl, an independent film producer, has summoned them to the conference room for a meeting. The current project is over budget, and he is fuming. But then, no one is surprised. As far as Darryl is concerned, the sun rises and sets on his countenance; he owns the moon and the stars. The crew is well compensated for their work on his film projects. But how can you put a price tag on missing a daughter's soccer tournament, not being able to attend an important meeting with a son's teacher, postponing a wedding anniversary, or, most of all, being abused on a daily basis?

Darryl is always late, even to his own meetings. He read in some book on management that the person who arrives last has the most power. This move is designed to make the statement that his time is more valuable than anyone else's. Darryl enters the room with authority. He is expensively dressed as usual, impeccably groomed. His face glows with a perpetual tan. After sixteen hours, there isn't a hair out of place, not a wrinkle in his suit. His straight white teeth gleam with a just polished look. Tall, erect, unbending, he stares into the exhausted, apprehensive faces of his crew. He begins with an explosion about a budget overrun. One man in particular is singled out for humiliation. The real blame belongs to one of Darryl's drinking buddies, who has a reputation for careless and irresponsible financial management. But the truth is of no importance. Above all, Darryl must protect his image and reputation and that of his friend. Darryl's attack is relentless and sadistic, leaving its victim and all his associates in a state of terror. Darryl knows he has won; his troops acquiesce once more. He strides out of the room in triumph, still king of his domain.

"Conversations" with narcissistic personalities are always one-sided: he talks; you listen. There is no give and take, no real interchange, no communion of thought or feeling. You are the captive audience. The narcissist erupts in a continual flow of information about himself, his accomplishments, successes, tributes. Bottomless and boundaryless, there is no end to the repetitive rhythms of self-reference. Like spring water rushing over the precipice of a roaring river, neither the space of a breath nor a heartbeat can disrupt the narcissistic flow.

Narcissists are walking advertisements for themselves. They name-drop incessantly, never missing an opportunity to tell you about their protean successes. Many of them are social and intellectual snobs who denigrate those whom they view as less educated, ill born, or culturally unsophisticated. Roger, a shopping mall magnate, attended a business dinner celebrating a world-famous architect. Expecting to be placed next to the guest of honor, Roger was chagrined to learn that he was seated next to me, the wife of the co-developer of the commercial project. I politely introduced myself. He appraised me with cold, dull eyes, as if I were some reprobate harassing him in a large public square rather than an adjacent dinner guest. He vaguely mentioned that he was a business associate of the main contractor. Throughout the dinner I made repeated, fruitless attempts to engage Roger. His form of communication was a series of verbal excursions into the hallowed world of his private contemporary art collection. He was effusive in describing his prized paintings in excruciating detail. He drooled over the clever schemes he had hatched to obtain them. I spoke of my love for classical art and my appreciation for the great European masters. Roger shot me a disparaging glance, as if to say: "You naive little twit. Don't you understand that these so-called great masters are irrelevant and passé?" Roger spoke to me as if he was correcting a small misguided child. His manner was rude and condescending. He spent the rest of the dinner regurgitating tales of his brilliant recent acquisitions. As soon as the opportunity arose, Roger bolted from the table to pursue other guests who would measure up to his level of aesthetic sophistication.

The narcissist takes up a vast amount of psychological space, leaving room only for himself. In his presence, one is unable to breathe or move; all the available oxygen has been taken up by his self-entrancement. At a business meeting or social gathering, he is the center of attention. There is no reality but his. Those who associate closely with this type of individual often feel that they are leading his life rather than their own and that his life is more valuable than theirs. When a narcissist turns his attention on you, the move is calculated. He has something specific in mind that will benefit *him*. You are a living conduit for the gratification of his narcissistic supplies—power, wealth, prestige, sexual thrills, adoration. These are the psychological foods that temporarily satiate the narcissist's voracious appetite.

When you meet a narcissist, he is asking himself, "What can this person do for me? How will I use him to achieve my goals?" A successful narcissist deludes others into believing that he is genuinely interested in them. It appears that you are the most important human being he has ever met. The target of such intense attention can be fooled by this charming scoundrel. When it becomes evident that you are of no value to him, there is nothing swifter than the narcissistic brush-off, sometimes subtle, often abrupt. What appeared to be a vital link with the narcissist has just been expertly severed.

## MASTER OF GRAND DELUSIONS

The narcissist lives in an intricate world of his making, dominated by inflated illusions of self-importance. His style is grandiose—like some peacock or wild turkey with feathers in full display. His version of reality bears no resemblance to the truth. Experiencing himself at the center of life, like a sun surrounded by encircling planets, the narcissist believes that everything flows from him. He is the first cause, the ultimate voice, the source of the river.

The narcissist fabricates delusions that protect his belief in limitless power. The narcissist holds fast to his bloated self-images, unlike flights of the imagination or fleeting moments of manic optimism that dissipate as passing chimeras of the mind. For him these are irrefutable and immutable truths. His core beliefs are unshakable: "There is nothing I can't do, I have no limits. I'm perfect—everyone else is mediocre and inferior. I will win at all costs."

The narcissist has an incredible sense of self-entitlement. Everything is about him and belongs to him. He smoothly oversteps the personal boundaries of others, mistreating, devaluing, and humiliating them to bend them to his will and his desires. He is the hunter; they are the prey. Like the dominant male lion of the pride, the narcissist knows that he deserves the first fruits of the kill.

The heroic narcissistic vision of self bears no resemblance to objective reality. The narcissist resides in a separate universe, keeping himself expanded like a human dirigible. Kevin, an orthopedic surgeon, was in the process of divorcing Sheila, his wife of twenty-five years. He had waited for this opportunity from the first months of their marriage. Once free, Kevin relentlessly pursued the next phase of his life with the younger woman he had been seeing on the side for some time. Throughout the divorce process Kevin acted with single-minded ruthlessness. He hired a "barracuda" to mine for legal loopholes and to keep his wife in a state of heightened fear. He fought every request Sheila made for fairness and conciliation. Kevin slapped as many legal and psychological obstacles in her way as he and his lawyers could muster. When the time for an equitable financial settlement arrived, he evaded federal taxes, lied about his true income, and seized the family home. Kevin was not only obsessed with winning the divorce battle but also with vanquishing his former wife. The reality that he had caused irreparable psychological and economic harm to his first spouse and their children never entered his mind. Only *Kevin's* wishes and desires mattered.

## A PATINA OF GOODNESS

Although he may be a malevolent human being, the narcissist believes that he is a "good person." Blind to his deceptions and cruelties, he automatically plays the role of victim when he is accused of iniquity. Willis, a media executive, had been married to his wife, Ingrid, for seven years. During all this time he had several mistresses. He called them his best wives. They adored him and always had time to listen to his flurry of ideas and plans. They were both compliant and sexually adventurous. He wanted to be free of Ingrid and the daily travails of family life. Willis hesitated obtaining a divorce because he despised the idea of handing over even a penny to Ingrid and his children. He was infuriated by the prospect that his financial resources would be drained. In his community Willis was revered as a self-made man, devoted to his family. Desperately dependent and fearful, Ingrid stayed with Willis. Eventually, she became clinically depressed and was required to take large doses of psychotropic drugs to function day to day. Willis continually undermined his children's relationship with their mother. He indulged them with gifts and special favors but was unavailable when they needed his time and attention. Despite his cruel neglectful behavior toward his wife, Willis's acquaintances and friends and some members of Ingrid's family viewed him as a caring father and husband. Willis had fooled almost everyone into believing that he was a "good person."

The pursuit of limitless individual power has become an aspiration and lifelong goal. For psychoanalyst and philosopher Rollo May, the narcissistic personality has grown out of an obsession with the individual and individualism—the need to struggle and succeed above all else. Each person must stand and fight the battle on his own and ultimately win over his competitors. This is the attitude, according to May, that supports and promotes pathological narcissism. He describes the narcissistic philosophy that now prevails: "The myth of success consoled us in the difficulties of struggling to 'rise' to higher and higher positions.... When we had a pang of guilt at exploiting our fellow men, we could whisper to ourselves that we need not take the responsibility for others, that they must learn on their own, and this expression of individualism then relieved us of our guilt."[19]

The epitome of this trend is the religion of celebrity in the entertainment business. Movie and television stars have become societal icons. Much of the public is captivated by every detail of their lives: marriages, divorces, adulteries, illegitimate children, sordid family secrets, brushes with the law. There is an exaggerated self-absorption among some celebrities in particular, reflective of a pervading narcissism that permeates the popular culture. Many of these individuals share the most intimate details of their lives, as if this information is profound or newsworthy. The cult of celebrity reduces the substance of life to empty trivialities.

The concept of limitless power is viewed as essential to private and professional success. Overemphasis on individual achievement has led to a culture of endless greed and cruel blindness to the needs of others. Rollo May describes these personalities: "The narcissistic patient . . . is the modern myth of lonely individualism. This person has few if any deep relationships." He is "the depressed 'man in the gray flannel suit.' "[20]

## THE WORLD'S APPLAUSE

High-level narcissists are handsomely rewarded for the very attributes that make them inconsiderate and demanding human beings: self-absorption, aggressiveness, hubris. This has occurred as a result of a devaluation of altruistic characterlogical traits over the acquisition of financial success, power, and fame. A substantial percentage of those who have achieved these new societal goals are narcissistic personalities. The public seeks them out as worthy role models. We are programmed to envy their success. They are fawned over and admired despite a delusional consciousness that rides high on the winds of self-adoration, outrageous demands, and excess indulgence. Receiving the world's applause is the shining jewel in the narcissist's crown. Setting himself apart from all the rest, he struts across the stage of life—cocksure. His ship leans at full tilt, all sails billowing, ego fully unfurled.

Opposite supernarcissist Pablo Picasso, Audrey Hepburn, the acclaimed movie star, did not suffer from this personality constellation. Thrust on the world's center stage, possessing gifts of acting, beauty, and grace, Hepburn conducted her life with authenticity, compassion, and courage. Despite her celebrity and artistic achievements, Hepburn always carved a distinction between her public role as an actress and her private life as a growing, loving human being. Audrey held no delusions; she aspired to live with clarity and goodness.

Everyone fell in love with Audrey Hepburn—those enormous expressive eyes with their perfectly curved brows, radiating a compelling inner light. Bone thin, lithe from countless disciplined years of ballet, Audrey became a film star almost by accident. Raised under Nazi occupation during World War II, Audrey faced the daily realities of imminent starvation and repeated horrific scenes of violent death. Her mother, Ella, a controlling perfectionist, demanded more of her daughter than was humanly possible to achieve. This psychological wound was apparent in Audrey's feelings of inadequacy and a belief that she was physically ugly. She resolved to work harder and longer than others, using her perseverance and will to make up for her perceived flaws and deficits.

With all of her professional success (an Oscar for best actress and five nominations), most of all Audrey wanted to be a mother. Her two marriages, the first to actor Mel Ferrer, the second to psychiatrist Dr. Andrea Dotti, produced sons Sean and Luca. Although these unions faltered and ended in divorce, Audrey devoted her time and energy to raising her children.

Throughout her life, Andrey was committed to alleviating the pain and suffering of others. For a number of years Audrey expressed her empathy for starving and sickly children directly though her work as a special ambassador for the United Nations Children's Fund, traveling to Third World countries.

Robert Wolders, Audrey's companion until the end of her life, speaks of her integrity and strength as she faced a painful and premature death: "She died not leaving anything unsolved.... She held no bitterness about her impending death, saying, 'It's not injustice, it's the way nature is.... It's the process.' "[21]

# CHAPTER TWO

# The Image Maker:

# Creating a

# Flawless Persona

*"She remained a long while at her dressing table. . . . She simply sat gazing into the mirror. And so in perhaps the truest sense she was at home, content at last with the half-glimpsed memories and dreams—with illusions of Marlene created and re-created for decades."*

— DONALD SPOTO,
*Blue Angel: The Life of Marlene Dietrich*[1]

## THE CONJURER

The magician displays his empty hand one moment, releases a soaring white dove the next. Now you see it, now you don't. This classic sleight of hand remains mysterious to the clapping audience. The glorious white bird appears out of the air from nothingness. Like the performer onstage, the narcissist is a conjurer, creating his magic by reinventing himself. The self that he perfects is his persona, that part of himself that he presents to the world. He mistakes this image for the real self, as he deludes others with his compelling charade.

Celeste wanted to be an actress since she could remember. She began to etch her finely crafted persona as a young girl when she changed her name from Susan Mae to Celeste. The name Celeste had a ring of drama; it made her feel unique, a stand-out. A gold-spun, sun-streaked blonde, with a gorgeous slip of a nose and large emerald green eyes, Celeste knew from the beginning that she was beautiful, a miniature star shining in the constellation of her family.

Even as a child, Celeste was fixated and mesmerized by her appearance. She adored having her picture taken. She stood in front of any camera, endlessly practicing a variety of facial expressions and body poses. She was thrilled with the eye of the camera fixing itself on her alone. Like Narcissus of the ancient myth, Celeste spent many hours gazing into the mirror. She was enthralled by what she saw . . . a perfectly symmetrical face that had neither a "good" nor a "bad" side. Watching herself in the mirror became an obsession. She was overwhelmed by her own physical beauty.

Unable to be true to himself and incapable of genuine introspection, the narcissist spins stories of an elaborate self out of whole cloth. If he has been told from childhood that he is superior to others—more handsome, brilliant, talented, gifted—the molding of this false self is familiar and natural to him. Like an artist who never finishes a favorite painting, the narcissist obsessively builds and refines a series of elaborate identities.

Robert, a computer sales executive, always felt superior to everyone he met. This sense of entitlement began when he was very young. Although he performed quite well in school, he was by no means a gifted student. When he didn't get straight A's, it was the teacher's fault. Although he was ordinary-looking, Robert was convinced that he was a very handsome man who could attract any woman he wanted. He viewed himself as sophisticated, worldly, and a gifted raconteur. Robert dressed expensively and meticulously. He told everyone that he owned his home, when the truth of the matter was that he had leased a house for the last ten years. He spent an unusual amount of time and money on his face and hair. Although he was only thirty-five years old, Robert had already undergone several plastic surgeries, including an eyebrow lift and an eye job. To achieve a razor-sharp jawline, he had liposuction under his chin to remove what he perceived as excess fat. He fretted over each new gray hair and arranged to have his hairdresser microscopically examine his head at regular intervals. During these sessions he insisted that the hairdresser dye even one hair that had turned gray. Robert avidly read books about how to become successful, including all the steps necessary to make a good first impression on others. He followed each step, like an actor practicing his lines, using specific phrases from these how-to books in his professional presentations. Everything about him was rehearsed and planned. He left nothing to chance. This way he was always in control of his image.

## IMAGE IS REALITY

Image is not reality. Yet today it appears to project great power. Image can be a beautiful illusion—a gorgeous young, lithe woman walking toward us; an exquisitely formed piece of fruit glistening in the sun; the curves of an elegantly designed car. In the last few decades the appearance of things has become a substitution for reality. People are judged more than ever by the external package that they create and how it is received by others. Age is a relevant example. Fifty years ago it was not nearly as objectionable for women in particular to show visible signs of aging. Today it is viewed as some exotic type of character flaw. The percentage of face-lifts has grown astronomically within the last few years. In some social circles it has become a necessary rite of passage for a woman to have a face-lift by the age of fifty. Many women are addicted to youth-enhancing procedures performed regularly by their dermatologists and plastic surgeons. A nip here and a tuck there are all part of today's accepted aesthetic landscape.

Many women (and men) are highly secretive about their plastic surgeries. I have sat across from many female acquaintances whose skin was so tightly pulled that I thought their faces would explode. They are compelled to undergo these procedures, even though there is the possibility of the job being severely botched. On more than one occasion I have encountered women, whom I have known for a long time, who present me with a visual surprise: eyes, brows, cheeks, and jowls are newly lifted and finely smoothed. Every facial feature is pulled to the limit, snare-drum tight. Not one word is spoken about the "work." These individuals believe that their postsurgical startled look goes unnoticed. There are others who simply appear one day looking "refreshed"—ten to fifteen years younger. They are giddy with the pleasure of their new façade. Some who admit to the procedures exclaim, "This has changed my life," as if they have accomplished some great deed.

Today, aging is no longer acceptable. Those who allow themselves to age naturally are considered defective. As the inner body systems go through their slow and inevitable process of decay, the face and outer body must project sensuality and newness. This is the latest commandment: "Thou shalt *not* look old." The addiction to cosmetic procedures emphasizes the externals rather than the inner, real self. The romance with the external image represents a pathological fear of death, the last taboo.

An essential quality of a great person is his persistent search for the truth. He uses his gifts not to deify himself but to contribute to the whole of life. A great man is aware of those who suffer and are in need and extends his efforts to alleviate and carry the burden that they bear. He lifts the spirits of those who are weak and desperate. He gives his time and attention unequivocally. He does *not* "pencil others in." By this I mean the common current practice of pretending to be attentive when someone is in trouble (financially, emotionally, physically) by producing all the right words and gestures. But when the going gets heavy and the extra extension of one's time and energy is needed, this person is nowhere to be found. Impatient and uninterested, the pencil-others-in folks are put off by the misfortune or tragedy that has befallen a neighbor, acquaintance, relative, or friend, especially if the situation is prolonged.

The great man is there for the long haul, the arduous ups and downs, the dizzying roller-coaster ride. He will not abandon the weak, ill, terrified, distraught, despairing, or financially ruined. His sense of time is not four or five precious minutes resentfully doled out. The great man is concerned with shouldering the pain and the burden while using the resources of his head, heart, and body to work toward a resolution of the crisis. He brings a sense of hope and calmness to an embattled individual, much like the loving mother who comforts her wailing child with her touch and tender murmurings long into the night until the storm has passed.

What is a great man? Who were and are the great men? There appear to be so few at the moment. These are the real questions. What is reality and what is illusion? What is the distinction between public and private, and where is the balance that we must find between them in a lifetime? Can we achieve in the world and be a monster in private and still be considered a great man (or woman)? Absolutely not! We must look at the microcosm and the macrocosm to understand the truth of an individual human being. There are no grace notes when we evaluate a life. Everything counts.

## THE PERFECTION OF THE EXTERNALS

The narcissist is always preoccupied with the impression he is making. This is particularly critical when he decides that he must win someone over to achieve personal gain or satisfaction. Narcissists are perfectionists. For some, everything in their environment—homes, cars, personal effects—must reflect a flawless self. Walking through some of these homes, I have wondered if anyone lives there. There is not one sign of human habitation: no footprints on rugs or carpets, no finger marks on furniture or mirrors, no body or cooking aromas or whiffs of faded perfume, no towel askew, no couch cushion indentations, no stain, no dust, no scuff, no smudge. I call this narcissistic compulsion "perfection of the externals." Every aspect of their outward environments must be kept in pristine condition at all times. Some people move from one lovely house to another again and again because they must have the next "new thing." There are others who continually remodel, spending innumerable hours choosing just the right color and texture of granite, wood flooring, paint. Doing, undoing, and redoing one's external living environment has become the centerpiece of many life dramas. Some individuals lead their entire lives exclusively on a surface level. They are incapable of introspection, the process of going inside oneself. Their focus is on the material. By this I mean physical appearance, professional and economic status, societal power. High scores on these indices represent a very successful life for these people. Their sense of identity is based on their achievements in the world or the amplification, exaggeration, or fabrication of these accomplishments. As Western society has become more narcissistic, the emphasis on material attainment as a basic life value has overshadowed the inner search and the journey toward greater insight and awareness.

Perfection of the externals can be achieved through one's children. A strong example of this occurs when a parent is unable to lead his own life. I know a woman who purposely met and married a surgical resident in neurology because such a marriage represented prestige for her and the perfect child she would produce.

George, the unwitting husband, never realized even after a long marriage that his wife, Gemma, had been using him to suit her narcissistic purposes. She would create a superchild, like an artist working slabs of clay into a masterpiece. When George completed his residency and was securely ensconced in private practice, Gemma deliberately became pregnant. As soon as this was accomplished, she quit her job and began her role as "the mother for all ages." From birth, Sophia was in her mother's company day and night. Gemma taught, coached, and trained her charge to excel in reading, writing, math, and several languages. She knew she was raising a prodigy. Sophia was both prodded and rewarded for her accomplishments. She was continually told how superior she was to other children her age.

Long before Sophia finished an elite private grade school, Gemma was already planning her daughter's university career. Sophia was psychologically fused with her mother and never really rebelled or separated from her emotionally. After giving birth to Sophia, Gemma began a pattern of completely ignoring George.

He was a source of financial stability, nothing more. A workaholic, he spent up to seven days a week in his surgical practice. During short spaces of time when he was not on call, he managed to have numerous affairs with nurses, administrative hospital staff, and other female physicians. Gemma and George were living in the same house but leading separate lives.

Gemma's entire identity was connected to Sophia's accomplishments. Gemma had no life of her own. Every thought, plan, and action was obsessively devoted to the perfection of Sophia. During Sophia's last two years in high school, Gemma began a high-gear campaign to get her child into one of the top Ivy League universities. She mined these fields through her friends and her husband's professional contacts. Gemma was consumed night and day, calling one person after another, studying every book possible to ensure that her prodigy would be installed in the "right" university. She contacted a distant relative who was strategically placed at one of the coveted schools. Twisting his arm, begging him, Gemma was able to get Sophia's applications and interviews seriously considered. At last her daughter was accepted to the university Gemma had chosen when Sophia was in diapers. Sophia went on to do graduate work in France. Eventually, she emigrated there. Mother Gemma visited her daughter often and kept in the back of her mind a plan to become an expatriate in France. This way she would always be near the priceless treasure she had created.

## EXPECTING EXCELLENCE
### FROM OTHERS, *NOT* ONESELF

Narcissists pursue women and men that possess certain attributes that they require to be a part of their unique oeuvre. In his personal life, the narcissist, male or female, usually chooses a partner or spouse who is physically attractive if not drop-dead handsome or beautiful. A narcissist would never purposely choose an ugly man or woman as a partner unless there was an ulterior motive.

In the current narcissistic climate, individuals who are physically stunning are highly prized. Flawless taut skin, symmetrical features, luxurious hair, distinctly beautiful prominent eyes, a perfect figure or physique—these are some of the aesthetic characteristics the narcissist is seeking in others. These become living, breathing narcissistic, ego-enhancing supplies, indistinguishable from the narcissist.

Besides outward appearances, the narcissist often picks talented people who will make him look brighter and more creative or clever. Naturally, he takes all of the credit for every battle won or accomplishment achieved. Those who live or work for him must perform beyond perfection. Regardless of his irrational, bizarre standards, the servant of the narcissist is expected to reach and exceed them. No mistakes or missteps are permitted. Although gravely flawed, the narcissist perceives himself as incapable of making errors.

Lizette's parents couldn't have been more proud when she was graduated with honors from a first-rate northeastern university. The summer after graduation she contacted an acquaintance whose mother was a high-level executive in television. She quickly obtained a personal interview through her connections and was soon hired as an assistant writer for a sitcom pilot. Besides extraordinary confidence and drive, Lizette possessed a striking physical appearance. She had taken all the courses at school that qualified her to write for this specific genre. She rose in her career as if she had been waiting for the opportunity all her life. While climbing the ladder, Lizette feigned a kind of humility and deference to her superiors.

She was competent, delivering just the right scripts when they were needed. She became known as an indispensable script doctor of characters or scenes that were not working. Lizette befriended Brenda, the head scriptwriter for one of the most popular and profitable television shows on the network. Brenda learned quickly that she could depend on Lizette to produce acceptable scripts on time without complaint or comment. Lizette kept her opinion of Brenda to herself. She saw Brenda as a plodder, a secondary player, a useful tool to ease her way forward. For several years she played a role as Brenda's obedient student. Finally it was time for Lizette to make her move. She began a smear campaign against Brenda, dropping carefully crafted remarks in the right places to the effect that her mentor had lost her edge, her writing was no longer as sharp and clear or even innovative and entertaining. Lizette made sure to speak to the right people, those who would be able to make decisions about the advancement of her career. She began a hot affair with one of the high-level bosses just to seal the deal. The following season Brenda was passed over and transferred to another department, where she would work on much less ambitious projects.

Lizette was currently the head writer for a top show. She luxuriated in her success. As her sense of entitlement swelled, she became increasingly difficult, a certified diva. Though often late or absent from meetings, Lizette demanded that her subordinates arrive early if they were scheduled to meet with her. She often spoke through her executive assistant if she didn't want to face some situation where she had made some critical mistake. Lizette played hardball with company executives, knowing that they would put up with almost anything to keep her. She knew precisely how valuable she was to the organization.

Lizette pushed her underlings to the limit—often screaming and shouting that they were stupid idiots and she didn't understand why she had to work with such "mental pygmies." Once she decided that an employee should be axed, she went after his planned demise with sadistic satisfaction. Lizette at times became physical with her complaints. She ripped up entire scripts, thrusting them to the floor as she screamed four-letter words at the top of her lungs: "This is not the quality product I expect. This is pure shit! Someone's going to pay dearly for such crappy work." Because she had become so indispensable in the minds of company executives, Lizette was deeply indulged and forgiven for her many inappropriate, clinically troubling, personality quirks. She came close to being fired several times but cunningly manipulated her bosses, pulling herself back from the brink. She felt triumphant, saying to herself: "You ridiculous fools. I've beat you at your own game once more." Lizette repeated her mantra: "I'm always right. What's the matter with you? I've never made a mistake, so if something goes wrong, it's your fault."

To this day Lizette continues her reign of terror, extracting high-level performances mixed with humiliation and fear from those who cross her professional path. She is not any easier or more understanding with those who share her personal life. Here, as in her career, she is careful to pick those who always feel like inadequate damaged goods, despite their redeeming human qualities. They sacrifice themselves, playing the role of masochistic victim to satisfy Lizette's delusional demands.

It is quite unlikely that Lizette, a narcissistic personality, will change either in behavior or character. Throughout her life, she will hold unrealistic expectations of others and make sure that they fail to meet them. No one will ever be good enough for her.

Beneath the bravado and grandiose actions of the narcissist we behold a psychological portrait that is dark, painful, and menacing. Backstage, the truth about this character is revealed in all of its deception, manipulation, and cruelty.

PART TWO

# *Behind the*

# *Perfect Mask*

# CHAPTER THREE

# The Exploiter:

# Deceiving Cruelly

*But what the fox hath once got in his nose,*
*He'll soon find means to make the body follow.*
— WILLIAM SHAKESPEARE,
*King Henry the Sixth, Part III*[1]

The narcissist is a master at extracting the pulp and juice of others—their time, talent, creative ideas, energies—to serve his purpose alone. When he has distilled the best from you and all that is of value to him, he discards the rest and moves on. *All* relationships with narcissistic individuals are exploitive. Believing that you have a real understanding with one of them is a blind illusion. Whether personal or professional, agreements, contracts, or covenants with narcissists are made to be broken.

Michael, an investment banker, and his wife, Marielle, an artist, had been married for fifteen years. Marielle was charmed from the beginning by Michael's extraordinary confidence and ambition. Everything he touched blossomed. He had a knack for making money. She soon realized that Michael was ruthless and cruel when anyone stood in his way. Despite his selfishness and insensitivity, she became habituated to the lifestyle that her husband's success provided—the trips, lovely homes, social access. For five years she had tried to get pregnant, unsuccessfully. At forty-one, she was very distressed by her failure to conceive. During this time Michael engaged in an affair with a professional associate twenty years his junior, while he professed his love for Marielle. When a sudden irresistible business opportunity in another state arose, Michael didn't hesitate. He abandoned Marielle, a sterile, aging woman who could never provide him with children. Within two years he presided over a thriving business, a young wife, and a new baby. Michael never looked back. Relentless greed and a desire to project a younger, sexier persona, superseded all the suffering and heartache that he left behind. Past chapters of his personal history turned as quickly as leaves moved by gusts of wind.

A narcissist doesn't waste time on those who cannot perform for him. By seduction or guile he draws to himself those who will feed his constant need for power and admiration. Narcissists use personal relationships as stepping-stones and way stations to success. They perpetually scan their environments, assessing their power positions, ever vigilant for those who will lead them to their next goal. The narcissistic personality values himself alone. Others are simply objects and vehicles who will satisfy his perpetual need for power and recognition. Throughout his personal and professional life, he betrays and manipulates everyone who crosses his path—spouses, lovers, children, business associates, friends.

The child of a narcissist must endure that he never had a real or loving parent. The mother or father that they revered and cherished was a counterfeit: on the surface, beautiful, handsome, charming, bright; on the inside, cold, disingenuous, enraged, empty. Many children of narcissistic parents struggle throughout their lives to obtain the love and acceptance their mother and/or father failed to provide. They suffer from the endless flickering hope that now or tomorrow or next year this mother or father will be different—capable of love. Some children idealize the narcissistic parent and strive to emulate him. This acts as a psychological defense against the intensely painful recognition that they were never and will not be cherished by this person whom they call a parent.

The narcissistic personality surrounds himself with individuals who act as extensions of himself. He fuses with those who will protect and expand his grandiose sense of self. When the time comes to discharge a member of the inner circle, he asks himself: "Is he of any further use to me? How will I dispose of him without causing myself any problems? Who is the replacement?"

As long as these supporting actors succeed in keeping their star shining brightly, the narcissist showers his blessings on them. Rewards take the form of money, prestige, professional opportunities, and special privileges. These blessings can be removed as quickly and abruptly as they were bestowed if the "master" is displeased or slighted. Those who work for or live with a narcissistic personality know that survival with him is always precarious. If luck holds and fate is kind, some chosen followers weather the unrelenting rages and demands that spill out of the narcissistic psyche.

There is always a time certain when a relationship with a narcissist will end. Followers are discharged when their gilt has faded. They have aged, become sexually and physically less attractive; their competitive edge is blunted; they have lost their slice of worldly power. Regardless of their years of loyalty and sacrifice, these faithful servants are coldly discarded, like trash thrown into a Dumpster. Eventually, calamity strikes; the hour of dismissal arrives. These are the moments when one is most at the narcissist's mercy—a little child cowering in the corner. The moment you cease to satisfy his endless ego needs, the narcissist will dispose of you. If you thwart him, he may destroy you. His capacity to wreak havoc on one's physical and mental health, reputation, personal relationships, financial status, can never be underestimated.

## DECEIVER

The narcissist is at all times a deceiver, never straight, clear, or true. He thrives in an illusive world of curves and meanders. He has mastered the ability to delude himself and others. Like a sorcerer, he hatches intricate plots in secret. He is the writer, director, producer, and actor of his unfolding drama. The proposal he brings to the table is never the "real deal." Like a seasoned poker player, the narcissist knows how to bluff his rivals, when to raise the stakes, and when to fold. Cold-blooded in his approach, he masterminds an end game that devastates his adversaries, leaving him intact.

Emotionally detached and isolated, the narcissist is incapable of truly caring for someone else. This callousness allows him to launch plans that psychologically wound others if he perceives them as a threat. In his obsession to win at all costs, he is unencumbered by ethics or morality. Hurt feelings, financial ruin, blighted reputations, incipient illnesses, broken relationships, suicides—are the tragic residue of the narcissist's endeavors. He leaves many lives in disarray and chaos, like bodies strewn on a battlefield. He coolly steps over these ravaged corpses to reach his destination. A narcissist cannot be loyal to another human being. The length of a relationship or its history is never a factor in how long it will last. At some point, determined by *his* wishes and desires, the relationship will come to an end. The narcissist will make his decisive move, leaving his partner, friend, or spouse bruised, battered, and abandoned.

Martin and Larry established a specialized medical practice several years after finishing their residencies. Using resources from their respective families, the partnership became successful within a short time. Martin was clever at attracting new patients. Socially gifted, a natural rainmaker, he spent a great deal of time becoming known in the community and establishing himself as one of its leaders. Although he was charming and appeared to be warm and friendly, this was a beguiling mask. Underneath, Martin was coldly ambitious. After several productive years, the partnership began to flounder owing to the growth of HMOs and the financial drain of several spurious lawsuits. Without telling his partner, Martin arranged to become the president of a large HMO. He abruptly informed Larry about his decision shortly before he planned to leave for a new position in another state. He promised Larry that he would always be available to support him through the transition period. Within a short time, Martin had vanished. The daily operation of the practice was left on Larry's shoulders. After several very difficult years, Larry was forced to sell the practice at a loss, and eventually he filed for bankruptcy. The financial ruin that Larry endured had a deleterious effect on his physical health. He never completely recovered either economically or physically from his former partner and friend's venal behavior. Martin thrived; he quickly and successfully became the president of an expanding HMO. As far as he was concerned, his former partner was a failure, an object of scorn and pity. Larry had become a bad dream, fading with first light, disappearing in the brightness of midday.

The narcissist puts his life in neat compartments that are sealed off from one another. He is able to activate self-identifications of vitality, superiority, success, and power. These are kept separate from the unconscious parts of himself that feel depressed, enraged, empty, and helpless. It is as if one side of the body is unaware of the sensations and activities of the other side. It is not unusual for a narcissistic personality to juggle a series of mistresses and wives with other peripheral affairs as well. Narcissists often have multiple marriages that produce different generations of children.

Practicing deception is common and customary among narcissists. These activities are viewed neither as betrayals of a marriage nor as psychologically damaging to a partner, spouse, or child. Donald, a plastic surgeon, had been married to Rita for only a year before he began an affair with Marilyn, a physician and colleague. Although his wife was pregnant when the affair began, Donald behaved like an unmarried man. When he was with Marilyn, the responsibilities of marriage and anticipated parenthood faded and dissolved. As the affair proceeded, Marilyn became more and more obsessed with marrying Donald. He kept her quiet by vaguely referring to a likely divorce in the future. Two years later he became irritated with her hysterical reactions and left her. A short time afterward, Marilyn committed suicide, leaving a note implicating Donald in her decision to kill herself. He was very upset—not because of this young woman's tragic last act but because of the possibility of public exposure. Even in the face of his former mistress's suicide, Donald was able to skillfully play the role of a happily married man with a loving wife and young child. He had mastered the art of compartmentalization, keeping those matters that could disturb him far away, locked in sealed, memory-tight, guilt-proof containers.

The narcissist cannot view himself objectively. Incapable of insight or self-criticism, he bases his identity on the illusion that he is unique, that there is no one in the world with his special gifts and talents. This arrogance combined with blind ambition permits him to follow a chronic pattern of deception in all of his relationships. Deceit is a part of him, like the length of his fingers or the cadence of his speech. If he was not deceitful, he would not recognize himself. Deception defines the narcissist as much as compassion and truth identifies the saint.

The narcissist is ruthlessly single-minded in the pursuit of his goals. No human feeling, concern, fear, or tragedy obstructs his purpose. He doesn't lose sleep at night over the human misery caused by his multiple cruelties. His underhandedness is deeply entrenched in the survival wars of childhood. It is an old weapon of defense against real and imagined enemies. As a child, the future narcissist learned that he must defeat his rivals at all cost and prove that he is a superior being. Deceiving them through seduction and trickery were the surest routes to victory. Along the way, this child learned how to win every time, even at the expense of his basic humanity.

A narcissist is a chameleon, taking on the shape, color, and texture of the environment around him. He is a facile actor, a quick study at sizing up a situation and turning it to his advantage. He is glib and smooth under immense pressure, especially when he is caught in a lie. A consummate actor, he plays his part masterfully, believing every word and gesture. When the curtain comes down and the spotlight dims, he leaves the stage and moves on to his next performance.

## GURUS OF "SPIRITUAL LITE"

A pernicious type of narcissist presents himself as a spiritual mentor. Attractive, bright, charismatic—these individuals flourish within a current popular cultural phenomenon that I call "spiritual lite." They practice pseudo-spirituality, presenting themselves as gurus who will ease your psychological pain, heal your physical maladies, and rescue your soul. Slick, smooth, and media-savvy, they write books, give seminars, and produce CDs, videos, Internet websites, and television presentations that offer visions of instant enlightenment, like a new brand of microwavable dinners. These narcissistic individuals are highly sophisticated and shrewd about human desires and weaknesses. They prey on the vulnerable who are lonely, have chronic emotional problems, or are bored with the monotony of their daily lives. Not so long ago, in his classic work *The Culture of Narcissism,* Christopher Lasch warned the West about these "teachers" and their rabid followers: "In a dying culture, narcissism appears to embody—in the guise of personal 'growth' and 'awareness'—the highest attainment of spiritual enlightenment."[2]

The gurus of spiritual lite fool most people. Many of them have stellar educations and glowing credentials on paper. They are physically attractive, socially adroit, gifted in the art of persuasion. The critical flaw is with their characters; they are narcissistic personalities, wolves in sacred clothing. These pseudo-gurus soothe and mesmerize prospective followers. They rely on the impatience of the restless, meandering Western mind, which is always looking for a quick fix to take away the pain. They assure you that you can keep your life just the way it is and still become spiritually evolved. They make promises: "Say this chant, repeat this mantra, gaze at that picture, and spiritual transformation will occur spontaneously, like a miracle. You don't have to be disciplined or give up any of your old habits or material desires."

Spiritual lite comes in a variety of packages: from plain brown wrapper to the most extravagant coverings, from a day's workshop to a sumptuous cruise halfway around the world, to an ashram filled with gold icons. The price of attaining pseudo-spirituality can be high, with charlatans and con artists becoming materially very comfortable as a consequence. The most successful ones create entire industries of "spiritualization." They proselytize through the constant flow of their DVDs, CDs, seminars, and retreats. Public speaking fees alone can land them tens or hundreds of thousands of dollars for a single event. I have seen the most sophisticated and educated individuals seduced by spiritual-lite narcissists.

True spirituality is the opposite of narcissism. Its purpose is to work through layers of delusion to the truth. Teachers on a spiritual path focus on you not themselves. An authentic spiritual person comes without fanfare; he is not waiting for the next closeup, speaking fee, or autograph. Genuine spiritual paths are filled with hard work, discipline, and supreme patience and perseverance. They contain many ruts, steep hills, and sheer cliffs. Spiritual progression is hard-won. The true guru is humble. He is attached neither to making large sums of money nor to becoming famous and powerful in the world. Spiritual lite will always be with us, as long as we believe and follow those who promise us peace and enlightenment as if it is a package of instant pudding—add milk and stir.

## CONTROLLER

The narcissist is a tyrant who controls the world that he creates. He holds absolute power over his subjects, who have no rights of their own. Like a dictator, he writes arbitrary laws that everyone is expected to obey. He appears to delegate authority. This is a misperception. He surrounds himself with associates who answer only to him. The narcissist uses an intricate collection of carrots and sticks with employees and associates as tools of control. He promises to handsomely reward those who fulfill his wishes and demands with money, prestige, and power incentives. He says: "If you do what I ask, you will be powerful and special like me." He holds up a high bar of expected achievement, beckoning prospective victims to play his game. When the goal is reached, the narcissist raises the bar and changes the rules. He sets up the game so that he always wins, and you always lose.

Irwin, a senior partner in a prominent civil litigation firm hired Charlotte as an assistant in his court cases. Charlotte was professionally well qualified; she had distinguished herself as a formidable adversary in the courtroom. Irwin promised her from the outset that she would share a percentage of the contingent fees from the cases she tried and won. Charlotte was a great asset to the firm and to Irwin in particular. Despite her success with all of her court cases, the promised percentage from Irwin was not forthcoming. When she confronted him, he explained that overhead expenses had increased substantially and that she needed more professional experience to earn her share of contingent fees. Irwin had made an agreement with Charlotte; she had reached the agreed-upon goal only to discover that there was no reward waiting at the other end. He had raised the bar, and set up the scheme so that he would always win and she would always lose. On a more cynical level, Irwin never had any intention of compensating Charlotte. From the beginning, he had decided to extract the maximum from her, using her talent and hard work to his benefit. When she became dissatisfied with this arrangement, Irwin would replace her with an eager young attorney naively willing to play the "raise the bar" game.

The narcissist is always aware of the end game—how he will dispose of a a partner, colleague, employee, wife, or mistress—when someone ceases to be of value. In his psychological world one person is interchangeable with another. The narcissistic personality adroitly finds a replacement who is prettier, hand-somer, younger, more amusing, smarter, and more exciting than the last. Like a lightbulb that has burned out, the once prized individual is replaced by a new and shinier one.

The iron grip of the narcissist's control extends to all the significant people in his life: spouses, lovers, partners, children, colleagues, employees. His grand plan is to perpetuate and maintain his personal and professional power. Those under his control are not free to lead their own lives, to make decisions and mistakes, to use their talents and energies, to have their own dreams. Their only purpose is to assist the narcissist in fulfilling his grandiose vision of himself.

The narcissist is a puppet master, pulling all the strings, deciding all the moves. The puppets come alive only in his hands. They have no power or influence by themselves. The master can bring a puppet into full light or leave him in shadow, remove him from the stage, discard him permanently, or destroy him. He is the ultimate authority.

The narcissistic personality controls others the way he was controlled as a child. The mother of the narcissist is often narcissistic herself. She projects on her child an image of omnipotence and perfection. She is incapable of accepting him as a distinct, authentic individual. She sees him through the distorted lens of the idealized image she has created. She remains tied to the picture of the perfect child she has molded. The child in turn never detaches himself from her psychologically. Mother and child remain tragically locked in an unbroken symbiosis.

Often very attractive, narcissists know exactly how to manipulate others. Combined with a stunning appearance and social polish is a compelling self-confidence. When the high-level narcissist focuses his charm on others, they feel more alive. He gives the impression that he understands you intimately and has your best interests at heart. This charm is seductive, containing a powerful sexual component. He communicates that "you are the most important person in the world. I know what you want, and I will get it for you." He is clever at discerning the narcissistic needs of others. He presents himself as a savior who understands your deepest longings for attention and a sense of specialness.

Those who are enchanted by the narcissist believe that he holds the magic that will lift them out of their ordinary, predictable lives. Everyone wishes at one time or another to be rescued. We want someone else to take over for us, to love us unconditionally, to give us whatever we want. The wish to be adored is primary and irresistible. It reaches back into earliest childhood, when we were dependent on a mother's love in order to survive. The narcissist, with his arresting charm and sheer force of personality, is capable of activating these deep wishes in others and in using his desirability to exploit them.

Sylvia will never forget the day she met Mike. It happened during a midsummer heat wave. She and her friends were sunning themselves at the beach. Sylvia went up to the refreshment stand to order lunch. She was aware of someone's eyes on her. She looked up and saw a tall, broad-shouldered, tanned blond man with beautiful cornflower-blue eyes. He gazed into her eyes, never blinking. Sylvia felt the attraction immediately. At twenty-one, Mike exuded tremendous self-assurance. Other young men were timid or halting in their approach. Mike spoke directly, telling Sylvia that she was beautiful and that he wanted to go out with her. She knew that Mike was giving her a line, but she wanted to believe him. He was so gorgeous and sexy that she couldn't say no to him. Shortly after their first meeting, Sylvia became intimate with Mike. As time passed, she found out that he was sexually active with several other women at the same time. Sylvia continued her intimate relationship with him, despite his deception. Every time she confronted him with his betrayals, he used his charm and sexual magnetism to convince her she was his only girl and that rumors about the other women were false. Mike knew he could get whatever he wanted with his personal allure. He had no genuine feelings for these young women. They were sexual objects. When the excitement of the chase waned, it was time to find and conquer the next challenge. More than the sexual gratification he received from these multiple sexual intimacies, Mike used these liaisons to fuel his grandiosity and inflate his sense of omnipotence.

Another narcissistic control strategy is based on assessing the other person's ego weaknesses—desires for status, material possessions, admiration, recognition. He holds out enticements that he has no intention of honoring. The narcissist works through intimidation, knowing that the other individual is too afraid and insecure to confront him. In some instances, he uses implied threats that force a colleague or underling to capitulate to his will. The narcissist is a street fighter, quick to size up his opponent's weakest spots. He thrives in a psychological environment of "kill or be killed."

## EASY LIES

Lies roll off the tongue of a narcissist as smoothly as butter melting on hot bread. For him, lying is as natural as breathing. Even a trained observer, a therapist, can be fooled by these lies. A lie is a handy tool the narcissist uses to enhance and protect the image he has so painstakingly built. Lies are automatic; they flow from him as effortlessly as sweat coming through pores. The narcissist often believes his lies. For him there is no ultimate objective truth, only his carefully crafted version of reality.

Most of us have difficulty lying, whether by omission or commission. Lying makes us feel uncomfortable, as if something is fundamentally wrong. We have a powerful visceral reaction when we lie. Our hearts race, we sweat, we get dizzy, and adrenaline pumps through our bodies. When we lie, we feel ashamed. We wonder if our perfidies will hurt someone else or put them in jeopardy. Some of us avoid lying only because we are afraid of getting caught. The narcissist is not burdened by this fear. He knows he can lie and get away with it. Lying for him is like a shortcut on a crowded highway. It is a free ride in the fast lane that will get him to his destination more quickly and directly than telling the truth.

The narcissist insists that the way must be clear for him to move ahead. If the path is smoothed through his lying, that's all right. He looks you right in the eye and lies without hesitation. He is glib with his lies; he shades the truth or tells an outright lie. He is a master at justifying lies to himself. Some people refrain from lying only because they fear retribution from an Old Testament God. This is not true for the narcissistic personality. He is shameless in his lying. He has priorities other than telling the truth. Lying for the narcissist is ego-syntonic, meaning that he is comfortable with this kind of behavior.

Narcissists lie through a mechanism called revisionism. They rewrite the history of an event, a contract, an agreement, or a relationship to secure their goals. They are particularly adept at reinventing their personal histories, creating heroic acts, even nobility, out of whole cloth. Like any good storyteller, the narcissist weaves a convincing tale that shades or perverts the truth. This story becomes his truth until it is no longer workable in supporting his aims. Famous narcissists write autobiographies that present their lives in the most positive light. These life histories are long and complex testimonials to self-aggrandizement. The infamous industrialist Armand Hammer wrote an autobiography replete with distortions and fabrications of his life calculated to enhance his image as a brilliant and great man. Many details presented as factual were the grandiose imaginings of a classic narcissistic personality.

Lying and evasion are a way of life for the narcissist. He exaggerates his accomplishments and minimizes his errors. He blames his mistakes on others, whom he knows are either too fearful or too dependent on him to protest. The narcissist uses stealth tactics and brilliant timing to disappear when trouble is brewing and magically reappear to receive accolades and tributes when awards are in order.

Sidney, a corporate attorney, shared the stewardship of an ailing company with two other executive officers. Although he contributed only minimal effort and time to his job, he held an influential position. He had been with the company from the beginning and harbored secret, incriminating information about their past and current financial affairs. He kept his power because he knew where "all the bodies were buried." Sidney had the gift. Like a man with bionic eyesight, he sensed trouble in the distance long before it reached his shore. He always slipped away to safety before the storm hit. After the trouble had blown over, he returned to home base, his power intact. In the opposite way, Sidney would appear like a stealth bomber out of the empty blue sky when bonuses, awards, or tributes were passed out whether he deserved them or not. He had honed his exquisitely timed comings and goings to a high art form.

The narcissist uses a series of lies and misrepresentations to diminish and destroy the careers and reputations of his rivals. He is as desperate to hold his power as a hungry leopard or cheetah looking for a kill. The narcissist lives in a state of constant suspicion. Friends can suddenly become enemies in his world. He is always on guard, waiting for the late knock on the door, the ambush, the stab in the back. Lying for the narcissist is absolutely necessary, a matter of life and death. In his deluded reality, there are no lies only expediencies.

## GUILTLESS

Children develop a sense of right and wrong from their parents. In the beginning, the young child idealizes his mother and father. As he becomes more separate psychologically from them, these idealized parental images are modified and become more realistic. A conscience develops over time as the growing child is able to take greater responsibility for his impulses and actions. The future narcissist never learns that there are moral or ethical limits to his behavior. His parents (mother and/or father) treat him like an extraordinary being—the most brilliant, creative, talented, handsome, beautiful child that ever lived—who is not subject to the rules and restraints placed on others. The parental message is: "You are perfect, you can do no wrong—anything goes." From childhood onward, the narcissistic personality preserves this picture of his omnipotence and perfection. Psychologically frozen in infancy, the adult narcissist is a small, petulant child trapped in the delusions of toddlerhood. He throws tantrums if he doesn't get what he wants. He cheats others if that is necessary to excel. He plots to destroy a colleague in a battle for a top spot. He'll betray an old "friend" without a quiver of guilt. While the previous friend spends sleepless nights wondering what happened between them, the narcissist slumbers deeply without worry or care.

Margo, a middle-aged television producer, had worked tirelessly to obtain her position with a major network. After years of eighteen-hour days and a constant struggle for professional survival, she felt that she had finally "made it." When her workload became unbearable, she hired Claudia, a twenty-six-year-old attorney and Ivy League graduate, as her new assistant. In the beginning, Claudia was obsequious, almost worshipful in her attitude toward Margo. She became deeply immersed in her job, surrendering herself to late-night and weekend hours. Claudia pursued Margo relentlessly. She learned all of the details of her personal life. She sat at Margo's feet and looked up to her as a mentor. Margo trusted Claudia and shared many confidences with the younger woman, to the point of becoming emotionally vulnerable. In secret, Claudia plotted Margo's professional demise. Over time, with exquisite calculation, she persuaded her superiors to put her in Margo's position. Margo was shocked and traumatized by her demotion. She was kicked upstairs and removed from the senior executive track. Claudia moved inexorably forward the way she had always planned. There was no glance back at her fallen former friend. The summit was in sight. Claudia was taking what she deserved. For her there was no guilt—only the thrilling promise of a bright professional future.

## ARMAND HAMMER: RUTHLESS MANIPULATOR

The word *ruth*, which comes from Middle English, means "pity" or "compassion." To be ruthless is to treat another person without mercy. Because of the narcissist's skillful use of seductive charm and refined social graces, it is difficult for most people to believe that a narcissist can be cold and ruthless. When he wants something from you, he is purposely disarming, listening to your every word, focusing his attention on you like a laser beam. He gives you a rush, a feeling of excitement as if the most wonderful thing is about to happen to you. Often successful professionally, the narcissist may impress you with the fruits of his elegant lifestyle. He might bring you temporarily into his inner circle to dazzle you. The accoutrements of his power are compelling, even thrilling. But this is the lure, the bait, the trap.

Armand Hammer was an exploiter par excellence. Industrialist and entrepreneur he thrived on the ruthless manipulation of others. His style, though thinly convivial, was direct and forceful: more sledgehammer than velvet glove. In his personal life he acquired and disposed of an endless series of wives, mistresses, and girlfriends. He used his collection of female admirers to enhance his image as a powerful, brilliant, virile man who automatically magnetized women to him. For Armand, marriage was strictly a business deal. Incapable of shame or humiliation, he used the monetary resources of his second wife, Angela Carey Zevely, to finance a monumental cattle-breeding business. Ultimately, their union terminated in an ugly domestic and legal battle.

Frances Tolman was a lonely, childless, and wealthy widow of fifty-three when she read about Hammer's acrimonious and very public divorce from Angela. Frances recalled that she had met Armand many years before, at a Hammer Galleries sale. She got in touch with him and offered her understanding and assistance. "Hammer, after ascertaining how wealthy she was, realized that there was something she could do for him: provide him with money."[3] Hammer put large sums of Frances's personal money into his various business ventures, including the financing of Occidental Petroleum. Armand purposely pursued Frances, sweeping this naive middle-aged woman off her feet. As Armand's third wife, Frances provided him with undiluted adoration and devotion. Frances served as Armand's quiet shadow and silent, acquiescent servant.

Armand made sure that he was never photographed with Frances, despite the fact that the two of them had been married for many years. He always insisted on being at center stage in the spotlight, where his audience would focus strictly on him. Frances seemed to accept her role by saying that she didn't like to be in the public eye. At a New York party celebrating Occidental's initiation onto the New York Stock Exchange board, Frances spoke matter-of-factly about Armand: "My husband has a profound instinct for knowing who's influential, wealthy, powerful, or famous. If you're none of those, he doesn't waste a second on you."[4]

Armand's true feelings for his wife, Frances, are dramatically played out in his behavior in 1987 in Moscow during a reception honoring three generations of Wyeths held at the Soviet Academy of the Arts in Leningrad. As Armand and Frances walked downstairs toward the receiving line, featuring Mikhail and Raisa Gorbachev, Frances slipped and fell to the ground. Without missing a beat, Armand abandoned eighty-three-year-old Frances, leaving her crumpled on the stairs, as he raced to have his picture taken with the Gorbachevs.

This mean, insensitive act, combined with an accumulated insight into Armand's true motives toward her, finally gave Frances the impetus to become psychologically and financially separate from her husband. She began by changing her will in 1988. "She disinherited Armand and left all of her own property and her half share of community property to her sister's daughter, Joan Weiss, with whom she had remained close over the years."[5] Another humiliation that emboldened Frances was her valid belief that Armand was continuing his ten-year affair with his current mistress, Martha Wade Kaufman, and planned to name her director of the Armand Hammer Museum. Despite her fervent desire for a divorce, Frances "feared what Armand might do even to an eighty-five-year-old woman whose usefulness had come to an end."[6] Frances achieved a certain independence from her ruthless, deceptive husband by finally leaving him. Sadly, her moment of freedom was short. Soon after, she became seriously ill and died. Hammer didn't make the slightest effort to see her during her last illness, nor was he present at her death. Frances was of no further value to him monetarily. He had never loved her; he had used her. By the time Frances was dead, Armand was long gone, on the hunt for future bouquets of ever-increasing narcissistic rewards.

For ten years, Martha Wade Kaufman, one of Armand Hammer's many mistresses, shared his affluent, peripatetic lifestyle. He purchased a love nest for her in Holmby Hills, California, where she was expected to "submit to the sexual demands of Hammer."[7] He provided her with a job and financial support and a promise that she would "never have to worry about money again."[8] In exchange for this arrangement, she was subjected to demeaning demands by Hammer. He insisted she change her name to Hilary Gibson and transform her physical appearance so radically that his wife, Frances, would not suspect their liaison. Hammer demanded that she "undergo various surgical procedures to facilitate impregnation by him—while he watched and directed."[9] She put her life in his hands and endured countless mortifications in order to participate as a supporting actor in the life of Armand Hammer: tycoon, art collector, supernarcissist.

Armand Hammer was a master at arranging business relationships that would lead to his reception of extravagant public accolades. At age seventy-two he decided he could become "a hero for all time"[10] if he donated money to the Salk Institute, leading to a vaccine that would prevent cancer. Hammer knew that this would lead to a goal he had pursued relentlessly—winning the Nobel Prize. Hammer pledged $5 million with the understanding that a research facility would be established in his name (the Armand Hammer Center for Cancer Biology). Rather than acknowledge the reality that the development of a cancer vaccine was long-range and extraordinarily complex, Armand created an annual symposium of world cancer experts. He told his publicist: "Once they're all in the same room, maybe they'll get Salk to hurry up and invent the goddamned vaccine."[11] All that mattered to Hammer was that this achievement would provide him with a source of unending veneration as the man who had made it possible to rid the world of a virulent killer. Hammer as usual did not live up to his part of the donation agreement. After he died, a large number of lawsuits were filed against his estate. One of them was initiated by the Salk Institute, which Hammer owed $1,447,200 in uncollected promised donations.[12] "Within a year, more than one hundred charities, museums, family members, and other individuals would make claims."[13] Hammer never intended to comply with his promises. As usual, they were empty. At the finale, Hammer had countless enemies and few admirers. His companions throughout life were manipulation and greed. He rode his final wave with the pomp and grandiosity of a decrepit bejeweled maharaja.

Ruthlessness begins with a pervasive insensitivity to the feelings of others. It grows slowly and surely in small, steady, almost imperceptible increments. It originates with the quality of the parents' emotional and psychological responses to their child—their unconditional demands for perfection, their chronic detachment, and falseness. The mother of the future narcissist is often adoring and possessive but emotionally aloof and highly self-centered. She treats her child not as a separate, unique human being but as an object that she can shape in her likeness. Some mothers of narcissists appear to be affectionate with their children and deeply attached. However, this closeness is based not on the child as a person in his own right but on the mother's narcissistic needs for approval, prestige, admiration, or power. As a result, the future narcissist is tragically divided between two selves: the outer shell of charm, grandiosity, and supreme self-confidence and the inner core of emptiness, rage, paranoia, and despair.

When ruthlessness runs its natural course toward destruction, it becomes treachery. Treachery is a profound betrayal of trust that causes grave harm to another human being. Treachery takes many forms; in the extreme, it ends life itself. Acts of treachery cause mortal wounds on the psyche that never heal, wounds that must be endured every day. Treachery tears a hole in our trust in life itself. After surviving this ultimate cruelty, we approach future relationships with doubt and suspicion. In the aftermath, we are always looking over our shoulder, waiting to be betrayed.

Treachery is the ultimate double-cross. It takes as many forms as there are individual personalities and life situations. We expect treachery among thieves and murderers. But there are so-called nice people who perpetrate treacheries. We think they are "nice" because we have misjudged them. On the surface, they are attractive, socially skilled, and successful. We are led to believe that they genuinely care about us. We mistakenly view these individuals through the tinted lens of charm, physical appearance, sexual magnetism, power, prominence, wealth, or status. This pretty package is a façade and a distraction. Beneath the impeccable, seamless image lies their true nature: cold, acquisitive, calculating.

Marcia grew up in a middle-class home, the eldest of two daughters. When she was age five, her parents went through a rancorous divorce. Her father had deserted the family several years earlier to live with another woman. He established a separate family with his new wife and severed his relationship with his ex-wife, Gretchen, and their children. After the divorce, Gretchen's bitterness and desire for revenge against her ex-husband and all men was communicated to the children, to Marcia in particular. From the time she was little, Gretchen groomed her eldest daughter for success. She often told Marcia that she was special. She saw in her daughter the fulfillment of her own thwarted dreams of power and prestige. Several years after graduating from college, Marcia began working as a personal secretary to Paul, a media mogul. She became acquainted with her boss and his family, and in a short period of time she was described as indispensable. Despite his professional success, Paul, at sixty-three, was bored and restless. Much of his dissatisfaction was the result of an unhappy marriage. His wife, Catherine, was reclusive and emotionally fragile. Within six months, Marcia began an affair with Paul. Marcia played on his emotional and sexual dependence on her. Gradually, she convinced Paul to leave Catherine. Paul and Catherine divorced. In the aftermath, Catherine was hospitalized for severe depression and was never able to put her life back together. With the ex-wife out of the way, Marcia could have Paul, but she didn't want him. She was incapable of loving Paul or anyone else (even though he adored her). Marcia now had what she had always wanted: unlimited access to wealth and the opportunities it bestowed. In the succeeding years, Marcia had Paul change his will, making her the sole beneficiary, disinheriting his grown children. She was immune to the pain and acrimony that this decision caused between Paul and his three children. It destroyed his relationship with them. Paul suffered from a weak character. He was terrified of losing Marcia, on whom he was completely emotionally dependent. Marcia, in effect, was saying: Choose between me and your children. If you decide that your loyalty is to them, I will go and never return. Five years later, Paul died, demoralized and broken, leaving Marcia his estate. She successfully fought off the legal claims made by his grown children. She was now a very wealthy woman. Marcia felt entitled; she had squandered precious, young, vital years ministering to a boring old man. It was time for her to be queen of the estate and scout for a new man: virile, lively, adoring.

The narcissist is predatory. Like a hawk in the distant sky, he circles and then suddenly swoops down to snatch his unsuspecting prey. Those who stand between him and his goals are imperiled. Using the weaknesses and frailties of his victim, he carefully chooses strategies that will defeat his enemy. All narcissistic personalities are cruel and sadistic. The perpetrator of treachery has murderous intentions. He may not actually kill his victims, but he finds undetectable ways to diminish or destroy their lives.

The seeds of treachery are scattered and sown in childhood. They begin with a lack of parental empathy. The child who becomes a narcissistic personality has been treated as an extension of the parent, not as a separate person. He is the perfect child, created in the parental image, not his own. Psychologically fused with the mother or father, he is at their mercy. The message of his childhood is "Be what I want you to be and I will love you; be yourself, defy me, and you will not survive." Eventually, a cold rage lodges deep inside this child, which no flame can warm and no heart can touch with love or compassion.

Our understanding of the narcissist's dark, tormented inner reality leads us back along the roads and pathways of his infancy and childhood. In the beginning, he was chosen to be the special one, the answer to his parents' inchoate and unfulfilled wishes, dreams, and aspirations.

# CHAPTER FOUR

# Golden Child:

## Growing Up as

## the Very Special One

*Her son was her Prince, and whether she actually told him
that his birth had been prophesied hardly needs to be proved.
Given Anna Wright's convictions, Frank Lloyd Wright saw
himself as predestined.*

— MERYLE SECREST,
*Frank Lloyd Wright: A Biography*[1]

## THE PROMISE OF GREATNESS

In many ways, the birth of the future narcissist is a second coming,
the fulfillment of all the hopes and dreams of the parents. Because
they feel empty and inadequate and are often narcissistic themselves, the child is the chosen one, the answer to all of their prayers.
In a family of several children, the special one(s) is picked for his
handsomeness or extraordinary beauty, athletic prowess, charm
and magnetism, intellectual brilliance, artistic talent, or some

combination of these qualities. In some instances, the budding narcissist is an only child or first child, the focus of attention in the household. A common message communicated by the parents is: "Everything we do is for you—you are the center of our world. We are counting on you to save us."

In normal psychological development, the infant begins life in a state of fusion and oneness with the mother. Gradually, by the age of two to three months, he slowly begins to differentiate himself from her. As time passes and he reaches toddlerhood, he asserts himself more and more as a distinct person—physically, mentally, and psychologically. The toddler is ambivalent about this separation. He struggles back and forth between the old dependency and his growing independence. With the help and love of a mother who always has his interests in mind, he slowly claims his individuality. About the time that the child takes his first steps, he is dizzy with a sense of omnipotence. He feels that there is nothing that he cannot do. There are struggles between his desires and wishes and the natural limits placed upon him by his parents. Along the way, mother and father teach their child that there are consequences to his behavior. The growing child gradually and at times painfully learns to deal with frustrations. The future narcissist never achieves separation from the mother (or father); nor does he acknowledge prohibitions on anything that he wants or chooses to do. Psychologically, he remains a small child, behaving as if only his wishes matter. Mother's (or father's) constant mantra of success and winning resonates in his ears. Slowly and surely, he is indoctrinated to believe that he is superior. The narcissist spends his life convincing others of his greatness.

These parents often choose a particular attribute in their child—beauty, intelligence, artistic talent—that demonstrates his extraordinary uniqueness. If he or she is beautiful or handsome, this quality becomes the focus of attention. A mother who feels inadequate about herself as a woman will fixate on her child's attractiveness to compensate for *her* flaws. In a sense, this mother believes that her daughter's beauty or son's handsomeness will make both of them desirable and powerful. Even as a small child, Natalie attracted attention with her striking facial features. Her mother, Deirdre, was obsessed with her daughter's beauty. Deirdre pursued a career for her daughter as a child model in magazines. Before finishing high school, Natalie signed a modeling contract with an international agency. In her travels back and forth, Natalie, now eighteen, met Ronald, a middle-aged man who was attracted to her physical beauty. Rather than encourage her daughter to finish her education or allow her time to grow up, Deirdre pressured Natalie to move in with Ronald. Within a short time, he began physically and emotionally abusing Natalie. Deirdre argued with her daughter to stay with him. She was much less concerned about Natalie's happiness and safety than her loss of status as the mother of a daughter who was associated with an important man.

On a psychological level, Deirdre had colluded in selling her daughter into a life of bondage and abuse. As long as Natalie was married to him, Deirdre benefited indirectly from the narcissistic supplies her daughter was receiving: social status and financial comfort. Keeping this marriage intact, vicariously fulfilled Deirdre's wish from childhood to be recognized as a person of privilege. In her mind it compensated for all the years of deprivation and shame she suffered as the child of poor working parents. Lacking the ambition, drive, or discipline to seek these accomplishments through her own efforts, Deirdre forced this pathological relationship on her child, despite the danger to Natalie's emotional and physical well-being.

# FRANK LLOYD WRIGHT:

## MOTHER'S PERFECT CREATION

From the beginning, it was clear that Anna Lloyd Jones favored her son Frank over her five other children. His sisters and his father, William, knew that from mother's point of view Frank "accepted his position as the be-all and end-all of her life with understandable satisfaction."[2] In his autobiography and stories about his childhood, Frank routinely distorted the biographical facts. He changed his date of birth from 1867 to 1869, as well as his place of birth.[3] These modifications solidified the myth of his specialness. Although he protested and fought against Anna's adoration, her worship of him created a self-image of overriding grandiosity, arrogance, and a marked insensitivity to the feelings of others.

Throughout his life, Wright felt strongly ambivalent about his mother. She was a constant and frequently unwanted monitor of his thoughts and actions. He turned to her as an ever-present ally in times of personal and professional difficulty. He knew she would always be there to champion him. At the same time, Anna was critical, temperamental, and controlling. Wright often felt the full weight of this maternal albatross pulling him down. During most of his life, he fought to pry himself from her sharp-taloned clutches.

Anna treated her son, whether he was a toddler or a middle-aged man, like her possession and creation. Early on, a tense psychological triangle developed and grew between mother, father, and son.[4] Frank perpetuated this family schism by showing favoritism and identification with his mother and disconnection and alienation from his father. Anna reinforced this dysfunctional family pattern by choosing her son as a psychological intimate over her husband. Anna "now loved something more, something created out of her own fervor of love and desire, a means to realize her vision."[5] She adored Frank and demeaned her spouse, William. Frank relished his role as a gnawing source of divisiveness between his parents. These family dynamics had the effect of making his father a diminished figure in the family tableau.

Before Frank Lloyd Wright was born, his mother, Anna Lloyd Jones, had already decided that he would become a master builder, an architect. From earliest childhood, she filled him with Celtic tales of a mythological hero named Taliesin, who had supernatural powers. Wright chose to call two of his homes Taliesin. This "betrays the force of [his mother's] early indoctrination since Taliesin is not only an actual historical personage but also a poet-savior, magician, spinner of riddles, seer and supernatural being."[6]

Taliesin is viewed as a figure capable of godlike feats beyond human scope.[7] *Taliesin* in Welsh means "radiant brow." It is no accident that Frank Lloyd Wright chose this name for his personal residence. He and Taliesin are intimately associated with one another. Wright explained that he had named his home Taliesin because it rested on the brow of a hill, providing a commanding view of the countryside surrounding it. A more likely interpretation is Wright's identification with Taliesin as the magical prophetic seer of bygone centuries.

Anna Lloyd's retelling of these Welsh heroic tales created a new family history that counterposed the brutal truth. The Lloyd Joneses came from impoverished conditions and low social status. Frank Lloyd Wright fiercely concealed the actual site of his real birthplace. He remained unpleasantly defensive about the time and place of his birth. If questioned, he became churlish and unresponsive. He could not bear to reveal feelings of shame surrounding his humble beginnings. Rather than stating the truth as a source of strength and integrity in illustrating his life story, Wright, like all classic narcissists, obfuscated the facts of his childhood. He compensated for these humiliations through a continual re-creation and embroidering of his autobiography. This shiny, new history began at his mother's knee as he listened to the ancient stories of her heroic Welsh ancestor, Taliesin.

The origins of the Taliesin character are fascinating. They begin with a village boy named Gwion Bach, who is commanded by the goddess Caridwen to stir a large cauldron.[8] When Gwion licks off three drops of the boiling liquid that have fallen on his finger, the goddess overtakes him and eats him. She carries him for nine months in a form of pregnancy and delivers the baby. She plans to kill him but cannot because of his extraordinary beauty. She spares his life by wrapping him in a leather bag and casting him into the sea. The following morning the village boy who has been reborn is discovered by Elphin, the son of a wealthy man. Overwhelmed by his beauty, Elphin and his companions call out: "Behold a radiant brow! Taliesin be he called."[9]

The constant reiteration and belief in these mythical origins and Anna's unremitting adulation of her chosen son stand at the core of Wright's development as a classic narcissistic personality. The Anna Lloyd Jones family proudly possessed the motto "Truth against the world."[10] Brendan Gill, an eloquent Wright biographer, modifies this motto for Frank to "Me Against the World with Mother Always Right Beside Me."[11]

Alongside her indulgence and favoritism toward Frank, Anna insisted that drive and ambition superseded the understanding and caring for others. Frank learned from his mother that empathy was not an essential ingredient of being human. Anna always made excuses for her son, allowing him to develop an automatic way of overlooking his many negligences and cruelties. This lack of empathy and a personality trait of pure callousness is clearly evident, especially in his personal relationships with his wives, children, and mistresses. Biographer Meryle Secrest perceptively speaks of Wright's "dark side: the ideal of himself as a misunderstood and persecuted genius encouraged him to see motes only in the eyes of others."[12] She continues: "It is safe to say that he was the most un-self-aware of men."[13]

The focus for Wright was always on himself as a true golden child, intrinsically entitled to do whatever he wished, despite the traumatic and tragic cost to others for whom he was responsible, even his six children. In a letter written to his mother after he had abandoned his wife, Catherine, and their six children and fled to Europe with his mistress, Mamah Borthwick Cheney, Wright complains that he is a victim of circumstances in a complex human melodrama. This is a typical ploy of the classic narcissist. He mercilessly injures others and then whines noisily that he is being persecuted. The golden narcissistic child, unlike most of us, cannot be tethered by the dictates of decency or morality or the thoughtful considerations that affect the psychological conditions of others.

Frank's emotionally charged relationship with his mother continued throughout their lives. He was joined to her as a finger to a hand, a leg to the trunk of the body, a heart to the chest cavity. He basked in the praise she heaped upon him and was especially impressed with her insistent belief that he was an unparalled genius without human limits. All of Anna's maniacal, dramatic energy contained a darker aspect. One of Wright's biographers describes her as "a pious, cold-blooded disciplinarian who fought to keep Frank bound forever to her apron strings."[14]

At Spring Green, Wisconsin, on a mountain overlooking the valley, Wright built his home, naming it Taliesin after the mythical Welsh seer and demigod with whom he so intimately identified. Here, he was lord of his domain. God help "the others" who dared to question how he conducted his life. This wish of the golden child, created and nurtured at his mother's knee, would now take shape and be fulfilled through the design and building of his refuge to self. In Wright's mind, the mystical Welsh hero and he were now one.

As Anna drew nearer to the end of her life, Wright was nowhere to be found. There is strong evidence that he was not present at her death and did not attend her funeral. After a lifetime of symbiosis with her son, she left this world without Frank beside her. Like a fish entangled in an intricately woven net, Frank was never able to extricate himself psychologically from the pathological bond with his omnipresent mother.

## COLD EMBRACE

Mothers and fathers of narcissists are often narcissistic themselves. These parents have cold and ruthless relationships with their children, based on manipulation not love and respect. Although these parents are often attentive to the physical needs of their children, they fail to respond to them emotionally. A narcissistic parent is incapable of empathy, the ability to understand or care about how someone else is feeling. The focus of the narcissist is selfish and insular. A life dedicated exclusively to self cannot encompass a genuine love of one's children. To become solid and whole, a child must be cherished for himself alone, for his precious individuality. When a child is loved in this way, he feels secure and grounded.

He is free to be himself no matter what the circumstances. He is capable of loving himself and others without guilt or fear. The care and understanding he received as a child is internalized, becoming a core part of him. The capacity to emotionally invest in someone else resonates through all of his future relationships.

The child who suffers the cold embrace is a puppet of the parent. In order to wear the family crown, he must relinquish the psychological essence of his true self, that part of him that thinks creatively and feels authentic. He must abandon the part of himself that is most alive. Mother (or father) is a master puppeteer who directs the child in *his* or *her* play. Responding to the parent's commands, under the expert movement of her hands, the puppet becomes animate on stage. The child puppet is captive to the will of the puppet master. He is not the author of his own life. The budding narcissist is an able pupil who learns to act convincingly in various roles. The parent rewards the child for mastering the play. After years of rehearsal and imitation, the future narcissist no longer needs prompting. He has mastered every facet of his many parts. He now waits in the cool, dark wings, eager to launch his starring role.

In some instances, it is the narcissistic father who offers his child a nonrelationship, devoid of genuine feeling or empathy. Allen, a television network executive, married Elaine, his fourth wife. She had two teenage children from a previous marriage, whom Allen adopted to provide himself with a built-in family. Allen and Elaine were highly social and entertained frequently. On most weekends, they invited company to stay in the main house. Allen insisted that the children live in a separate residence on the property. He displayed a formal affection toward the children but didn't really love them. He provided for their physical and educational needs. He expected them to have perfect grades, and when they didn't measure up, he devalued them with sarcastic remarks and gratuitous attacks. The children served as narcissistic supplies that offered Allen an image of devoted father and family man.

Although Allen encouraged his stepchildren to succeed, he did everything possible to make sure that they could never compete with him. He discouraged them from seeking careers in his business—entertainment. He made it clear that he would not use his influence to help them professionally. While Allen spoke of his stepchildren to his business associates and social circle in glowing terms, extolling their academic and athletic achievements, he didn't hold any real affection or concern for them. Elaine appeared to be devoted to the children, but she abdicated her role as mother in exchange for living in the reflected light of her husband's success. Even with every material possession at their disposal and all educational roads open to them, these children were psychological orphans, absent a true mother and father.

The parent who lacks empathy may provide every earthly advantage and fail his child completely. This parental relationship is not based on any real closeness but on a cold embrace. For some of these parents, rearing children is like a business arrangement. The child is never understood or appreciated for his own sake. He cannot go to his mother or father for comfort or emotional support. He is valued or demeaned, depending on how brilliantly he performs. The child is controlled by the parent puppeteer, who expertly moves the strings to satisfy *his own* thirsty ego.

An essential part of the cold embrace involves the exploitation and manipulation of the child. Though the narcissistic parent may appear to be devoted, he thinks only of himself. He sacrifices his child on the altar of fulfilling his own needs. Laura, a successful professional woman, highly accomplished in her field, had insisted since early in life that she didn't want children. She enjoyed her own company and those chosen few who graced her social circle, and did not want to be interrupted and intruded on by a needy, dependent infant. At age forty and with many romantic relationships behind her, Laura relished her freedom and never expected to marry. Quite by accident she attended a college reunion and reacquainted herself with an old boyfriend. After dating briefly, Laura and Arthur married. Within a year she unexpectedly became pregnant. Very reluctantly, Laura decided to have the baby. She returned to work six weeks after the birth of her daughter, Amy.

Although Laura spent very little time with Amy (she was cared for by a series of nannies), she had very specific ideas of how her child should be raised. As a little girl, Amy looked up to her mother, viewing her as some kind of superior being. Laura divorced Arthur when Amy was an infant. He disappeared and had no further influence in his daughter's life. Although Laura spent most of her time at the office, she always left detailed instructions on how Amy should be handled. Amy was an obedient, compliant child. Deep inside, she was afraid of expressing any of her own true feelings, since this would mean that she was defying her mother. She feared that any confrontation with Laura would reap harsh disapproval, humiliation, and emotional neglect. She had already lost her father. She couldn't afford to be abandoned again. Amy believed that she had to go along with Laura; if she complied, her mother wouldn't leave her. A child who is manipulated in this way doesn't feel real. She suffers from an intractable emptiness. She may be beautiful and bright and talented, but inside she feels like a fraud. All of her life Amy will suffer from the wound of maternal deprivation, which leaves a psychological hole at the heart's core.

In the beginning, mother and infant are inseparable, an island unto themselves. In the first months, the tiny baby cannot distinguish himself from his mother; his entire world revolves around her. This is a natural and necessary psychological state called symbiosis. The unique fusion between mother and child exists to guarantee the baby's physical and psychological survival. In the womb, the mother nurtures her baby through her own body. In the months after birth, the mother's role is to provide a secure, safe, calm, and protected physical and emotional environment for her infant. The adequate mother is exquisitely tuned into her child. The special sounds and gestures that communicate his hunger, frustration, pain, joy, and distress are recognized and responded to by her in unique ways that satisfy his needs. When he cries with hunger or fear or loneliness, she is there to minister to him. There are expected lapses when mother cannot attune herself perfectly to her baby. These minor interruptions in the baby's care teach him in small increments to temporarily postpone the immediate satiation of his needs. Through the weathering of these benign frustrations, the growing child comes to understand that mother is coming and, in the meantime, he can depend on himself. When the baby smiles, coos, and laughs, mother is watching and reinforcing his positive responses to himself and his world. She is the loving witness and caretaker. With consistency and time, these positive maternal patterns are internalized in the child's psyche, nervous system, in all his cells.

The course of the baby's psychological birth begins in the first cycle of separation from the mother around the age of two to three months. This process is slow and subtle. The baby starts to differentiate between himself and his mother, to make the distinction between what is "me" and what is "not me." His world expands beyond her body. When mother is not physically present, he is able to evoke her image in his mind and feel safe and comfortable. The capacity to internalize the mother takes place over time and is not complete until age three or four. The adequate mother is capable of separating her needs from those of her baby. She makes every effort not to place her wishes and desires first. As the child progresses, he learns to actually and psychologically walk farther and farther from her as he secures an intact separate self. Inside of him reside the imprints of all of his maternal nurturing—the capacity to calm himself, to feel whole, to control his moods, to be comfortable alone, to harbor a feeling of inner strength. He is becoming a solid self, a person in his own right.

The mother (or father) of the future narcissist has another agenda. She (or he) experiences her child as part of herself. The symbiosis that began at birth is never severed. Maintaining this unbroken union serves the narcissistic needs of the parent. As a result, the child is profoundly injured psychologically. When the mother pursues her own egotistical needs for extraordinary attention, recognition, and praise, she impairs her child's growth. In a contradictory fashion, the child is viewed as her saving grace, more vital to her than spouse, relatives, or friends. The mother's unconscious belief is that through him she will achieve the special status to which she is entitled. With the maintenance of this unbroken union, she redefines her sense of personal power while conjointly sharing in her child's glory and perfection.

This parent is often seductive with his child. In some instances, the natural erotic tensions between parent and child are accentuated.

The mother of a narcissist is often more attached to her son than to her husband. She idolizes the son and turns to him for a level of closeness that she cannot find in her spouse. Psychologically, the son becomes a marital partner who will fulfill her longings for intimacy and emotional gratification. Although no actual incestuous acts have occurred, the exaggerated erotic tie between them disrupts the child's growing personality. The seductive quality of this union diffuses the child's sexual identity. The narcissistic man cannot love women; he both hates and fears them. In his relationships he chooses women who are emotionally dependent on him and whom he can completely control. He interacts with women in a callous and demeaning way. The narcissist, as child and adult, hides a dark hatred for his exploitive mother. He despises the mother who tied him to her with seductive adoration and secret manipulations. He is trapped. Like a small animal caught in the lethal grip of a predator, he cannot extricate himself from mother's deadly embrace. This pathological fusion can also occur between father and daughter.

Sheila, the CEO of her own software company, thought of her father, Alex, as her only parent. Alex was his daughter's source of inspiration. He projected an image of self-confidence, absolute control, and personal power. She was awed by his extraordinary drive and irresistible charm. Deep down she idolized her father and hated her mother, Barbara. She had always been jealous of her mother's intimate role with her father. As a child, Sheila threw tantrums designed to keep them apart. She insisted on sleeping in their bedroom. Barbara suffered from a variety of psychosomatic illnesses, many of them perpetuated by the extreme stress of Alex's chronic sexual betrayals. Sheila viewed her mother as sickly, dependent, and weak; she despised her for these traits. Much of this hatred was fueled by her father's disrespectful and demeaning treatment of Barbara.

Although Alex was often away on business, when father and daughter were together, he focused an extraordinary amount of personal attention on her. Sheila believed that he preferred her to his wife. Alex reinforced the erotic feelings between himself and his daughter. He took her to grown-up places, like horse races and gaming establishments, when she was very young. Sometimes Sheila traveled on business with her dad. She often imagined that her mother would permanently disappear and leave Daddy all to herself. Sheila viewed her father as her hero, even her mate. She was incapable of acknowledging who he truly was—a ruthless, manipulative narcissist.

Although Sheila appeared to be professionally successful, her personal life with men was a disaster. She chose dependent men who offered the adoration she expected. She quickly grew tired of each one, disposing of them without ceremony. Sheila had a lifelong pattern of initiating adulterous relationships, repeating her father's destructive patterns with women. Sheila reveled in the thrill of taking another woman's man. She felt triumphant each time a married man came under her spell. These affairs were intensely exciting to Sheila. In them, she fulfilled her unconscious childhood wish of taking the wonderful Daddy away from the weak bad mother. Sheila spent her life playing the role of the "other woman." In childhood, Sheila felt sought after by a seductive father. Alex had placed her above his wife. He had offered her sexual closeness, which ended in disillusionment and frustration from which Sheila could not free herself. In the end, she played a ravenous man-hunter, trapped by her father's unfulfilled erotic promise.

When we make eye contact with babies, we experience them directly in a way that is both startling and refreshing. We look into their eyes and feel known on an intimate level. Babies disarm us with their realness. Psychoanalyst and pediatrician D. W. Winnicott coined the term "True Self": "Only the True Self can be creative and only the True Self can feel real."[15] Babies don't pretend. They are neither perpetuating nor protecting an image. They experience life fully in the present moment. A healthy, happy baby is naturally spontaneous. He laughs, cries, verbalizes, gurgles, gestures in response to his own body and mind and to the world around him. The adequate mother appreciates her baby's unique responses. She makes loving sounds and gestures in return. She communicates the message "I know and love you for yourself." The empathic mother doesn't impose herself on her child or force him to react in certain ways that aren't his own. She simply loves her baby for his unique self.

If the earth trembles in the presence of the narcissist, this isn't because of his authenticity or force of character. Rather, these are the stirrings of the grandiose False Self. Like the giant in the story of Jack and the Beanstalk, the rumblings of the narcissist can be heard throughout the kingdom. The narcissist at the core is a False Self obsessed with ego and image. The origins of the False Self begin with a mother (or father) who is unable to recognize and accept her child's individuality. Winnicott describes how the mother creates a False Self in her child: "The mother who is not good enough . . . repeatedly fails to meet the infant gesture [the infant's unique spontaneity]; instead she substitutes her own gesture which is to be given sense by the compliance of the infant. This compliance . . . is the earliest stage of the False Self, and belongs to the mother's inability to sense her infant's needs."[16] Rather than value her child as a separate, precious person, the inadequate mother insists that he echo her responses rather than his own. The False Self of the narcissist grows insidiously. As a result, he is incapable of expressing genuine emotions, particularly those that demonstrate the slightest hint of warmth or vulnerability. In a vital sense, a narcissist is not truly human. He is incapable of deep emotions—sorrow, joy, tenderness, love, remorse. A high-level narcissist is a supreme actor who fakes emotion brilliantly. He fools most people. Each move is carefully studied and choreographed to elicit positive reactions from others. He may even believe what he is feeling at the time. However, these feelings are fleeting and pass away as quickly as clouds rolling by.

Being real begins with a sensorimotor aliveness in the body. Babies and young children are present in every way. Their sounds and movements flow naturally. The narcissist is false at all times. Even when he is "sincere," he is false. He is practiced, a person playing a part. The narcissistic personality is the central figure in his own drama. The role that he writes for himself is brilliant and masterful but disingenuous. He struts across the stage, savoring each line. Many narcissists are handsome or beautiful. Some appear to have perfect bodies or faces (often maintained by multiple plastic surgeries). On closer glance, their bodies are hard and rigid, their faces unwrinkled and immobile. We watch them at a distance with a certain awe, admiring their flawlessness. Unmovable and unmoved, they are living mannequins. Their bodies stopped feeling long ago; their faces, taut and shining, are beautiful and handsome but blank, vapid, and emotionless.

From her earliest memory, Adela revered her mother. She was a physically striking woman who wore the loveliest clothes and

had a refined sense of style. She ran her home with meticulous ef-
ficiency. When her two children came along, Eileen promised herself that she would raise them as flawlessly as she had always
conducted her life. Her first child, Adela, showed early talent for
singing and dancing. She was taken to the finest teachers, and soon
was doing commercials and performing on the stage. Eileen presided over her daughter's career every step of the way. When Adela became a teenager and went through a physically awkward
stage, Eileen insisted that she have plastic surgery on her nose to
make it smaller and more aesthetically pleasing. Adela felt very
conflicted by her mother's decision to change her face. If she kept
her original nose, she would displease mother and possibly lose
her love; if she had it surgically changed, she would sacrifice a vital
part of her identity. In the end, Adela capitulated and had her nose
surgically reshaped. Eileen, a narcissistic personality, was fulfilling
her dream of redoing her child into her own image and likeness.
The fact that her mother's act of selfishness was immensely traumatic to Adela was overridden by her desperate need to present
the world with a beautiful and talented daughter. The narcissistic
mother attempts to extract from her child what *she* needs to feel
special. She plunders her child's soul.

Many of us who are *not* narcissistic personalities have internalized some of the qualities of a False Self that seeks to please and
charm others to get what we want. For the purpose of psychological
survival, we learn to adjust our behavior to parental expectations. When the False Self takes over the personality, the real
person inside is suffocated by all the "shoulds" and "should nots"
imposed by the parents. As babies, we are raw and spontaneous.
This is followed by a period of learning how to adapt to the world
so that we will be accepted and cared for by others. In many individuals, the False Self overshadows the genuine personality. When

this happens, we live in an illusion, donning a series of elaborate masks throughout life. When the empty masquerade becomes too painful to bear, some of us remove our masks, go deep inside, revealing to ourselves and others who we are and always have been. The cycle is complete: from real to false to real.

There are wide variations among people with regard to being true to themselves. The narcissist resides within a self that is not only false but highly deluded. The self-assurance of his omnipotence and his sheer personal force provide a fertile environment for convincing others of his superiority. For the narcissist and his sacred circle, he has transcended the human sphere to become a god.

The narcissist is a magician, a master of the art of deception. His confidence and charm draw others into his delusional world. A trickster in the shadows, he weaves intricate plots of betrayal and treachery that ensure victory. He appears to be invincible. But this is an illusion. Beneath the perfect mask of grandiosity and self-entitlement lies a tormented soul—empty, enraged, despairing, paranoid.

# CHAPTER FIVE

# The Well of Emptiness:

# Harboring Rage and Envy,

# Paranoia and Despair

*In narcissistic personalities the experience of emptiness is most intense and almost constant. In these cases, emptiness, restlessness, and boredom constitute . . . a baseline of pathological narcissistic experience.*

— OTTO KERNBERG, M.D.,
*Borderline Conditions and Pathological Narcissism*[1]

Who could be luckier? We ask ourselves this question, witnessing the extraordinary ease of the narcissist, privileged in every way. Fame, power, status, and success surround him like a birthright. He is a rarefied creature, an exotic bird, who deserves more than the rest of us. We view him with a twinge of envy. He satisfies his cravings and desires; he has no limitations; he is admired by everyone. It all seems unfair. We wonder: "What's the matter with me? Why don't I measure up? Am I so defective or weak or unlucky that I don't deserve more?

Why is his life exciting and full and mine so dull and mediocre? No matter how hard I work I cannot succeed the way he does."

The narcissist is never at peace. Quiet and contentment evade him. His engines of cunning are always at work. He leads a life of restless, compulsive activity. The narcissist is always in a race that he must win. He competes in every arena—sports, sex, business, social status, material acquisitions. If he is a millionaire, he must become a multimillionaire, even a billionaire. If he is vice-president, he must become president. If he has one lovely home, he needs to make it larger and grander. One house is not enough; he must own several more. His vacations are luxurious jaunts designed for self-indulgence and future elaborate storytelling and name dropping. Beneath the restlessness lies chronic boredom. The narcissist cannot just "be." He is incapable of quiet reflection or insight. He marches relentlessly forward, doing his special life's work—demonstrating how wonderful he is.

Hour by hour and minute by minute, the narcissist seeks ways to stave off his emotional thirst. Inside, his well is always dry. He must constantly turn to the external environment to get the life-sustaining water that he needs to survive—praise, recognition, sexual conquests, power. To achieve this, he chooses dependent individuals who continually quench his psychological thirst with compliments, accolades, and blind loyalty. Many narcissists provide themselves with sumptuous lifestyles that convey to everyone that they have "made it." The narcissist selectively chooses others who will resonate with his vision of self. He devises an ongoing array of rewards that continually feed his ego with the persistence and predictability of an IV drip.

Like a hungry wild animal, the narcissist searches his environment for sustenance. His psychological foods are admiration, wealth, power, fame. Without these ego gratifications, he feels diminished, even dead. He meticulously constructs an entire life-style that supports his distorted beliefs. Narcissists are constantly on the hunt, stalking the tall grasses for game that will satisfy their enormous appetites. As soon as he satiates himself with one reward—money, power, luxuries, tributes, honors—he is hungry for the next. The successful narcissist creates an intricate system of positive feedback in the form of friends, associates, partners, spouses—who perpetually fulfill his endless needs. When the sources of these ego rewards become unavailable or fail him, the narcissist experiences intense feelings of emptiness.

The narcissist's experience of emotional emptiness is beyond longing or sadness. It is a severe and intractable wounding, a pain so savage and deep that it seems intolerable. The psychological landscape of the narcissist is bleak. He has no inner resources to sustain him. He cannot turn to himself or others for real affection or solace. Although he enjoys the transient loyalty of dedicated followers, no one really cares about him. The narcissist feels empty because he is completely alone. Like a house without furniture or a landscape without vegetation, his inner world is devoid of meaningful relationships. All signs of life have dis-appeared.

Narcissists indulge themselves extravagantly. They have no dif-ficulty taking extended vacations, owning enormous houses, buying the newest private jets. It is almost impossible to imagine the level of excess that these individuals attain. They build immense monu-ments to themselves that contain more square footage than many public buildings. Narcissists support huge entourages that are on call twenty-four hours a day to respond to their every need—physi-cal, emotional, sexual, spiritual. They host parties that cost in the millions and are given principally to display and demonstrate their exceptional social and financial status.

Narcissists keep score. They watch rivals with microscopic vigilance. A narcissistic billionaire is envious of a multibillionaire. It is difficult to imagine a rivalry among billionaires, but this is the rarefied world of competition among the most successful narcissists. This does not mean that all billionaires or millionaires are narcissistic. Wealth alone or lack of it are not determinants of a diagnosis of narcissistic personality disorder.

The extremes of narcissistic acquisitiveness are startling. Candace had been married to Antoine, a vascular surgeon, for three years. The third of his wives, she was, at thirty-eight, the youngest, and the most beautiful. She enhanced Antoine's image as a successful, virile, attractive man of sixty-five. The couple led privileged lives. They owned three magnificent houses and several vacation hideaways. They took frequent cruises. Candace's need for self-care went far beyond that of her friends, social acquaintances, or anyone else. She secretly and compulsively shopped daily in the fanciest stores. She hired private chefs to prepare their daily meals. Terrified of looking older (she told everyone that she was twenty-eight), she built an elaborate home spa and hired a staff of beauticians, personal trainers, dieticians, and masseurs to attend to her beauty needs around the clock. Every month Antoine was deluged with large credit card purchases for luxury items and personal-care services. He became furious with Candace but forgave her quickly. She resumed her excessive spending and her endless cycle of indulgence, satiation, and craving.

Certain professions by their nature (movie, television, and stage actors; models; professional athletes; politicians) offer a continual supply of ego food. With their emphasis on the outward image and performance (beauty, handsomeness, youth, sexiness, athleticism, desirability), these occupations attract narcissistic personalities. The exhibitionistic nature of their work provides narcissists with unending opportunities to reinforce their vanity and activate their grandiosity. They are surrounded by a built-in audience, always clapping and smiling. Entertainers (stage, screen, television) are the recipients of a constant stream of adulation. The audience sitting in the dark identifies with the actor in the spotlight. We idealize entertainers as we watch them perform. We fantasize about their personal lives. We put our wishes and desires into them. Some entertainers are worshiped. Our narcissistic society encourages the veneration of entertainers by raising them to the status of cultural royalty.

There are actors who feel truly alive only when they are on-stage. They believe their press clippings, adoring fans, and glowing reviews. When the applause stops, particularly when they are old and the best roles are no longer forthcoming, the sense of emptiness becomes overwhelming. As the external attractiveness drops away and he is no longer sought after, the narcissistic actor recedes and withers into a dying shell.

Politicians are entertainers. Their stage is the political arena, their audience, the voters. They perform in Washington, in their districts, while campaigning and during the twenty-four-hour news cycle. Politicians are constantly activating their egos. With the emergence of a ubiquitous media, the temptation for politicians to perform rather than serve has become too great to resist. In front of the cameras and on the campaign trail, the narcissistic politician feels energized and inflated. He is stage center, the person everyone comes to see. His emptiness is continually filled by the approving attention of his constituents and the mass audience.

The narcissist manufactures elaborate escapes designed to obliterate his feelings of emptiness. One method of flight is the sexual affair, a shallow relationship that creates instant diversion.

Many narcissists are compulsive womanizers who use sex as a drug to keep themselves feeling both physically and psychologically potent. Male narcissists often have a series of mistresses and girlfriends. When life with their wives becomes boring, they turn to other women to fill the void. What better way to distract oneself than to be in the arms of an always available adoring lover. Narcissists are often sexual thrill seekers. They keep several women (or men) on the string at a time, expertly dodging jealous husbands and wives. The possibility of getting caught heightens their sexual arousal.

## BOTTOMLESS RAGE

"Her outburst took my breath away. I felt my adrenaline pumping all day long after her screaming fit. I was waiting for the other shoe to drop." Stacy is describing her experience as an employee of Nadine, the owner of a wedding consultant service. Nadine had a reputation for putting on idyllic weddings. Stacy had been offered an apprenticeship with Nadine's company. Stacy revered Nadine from a distance; she had been reading about her mentor for years. She knew that the opportunity to learn from an expert would further her professional career. At first Stacy thought she was blessed. Nadine was bright, confident, and talented. Stacy shared all of her creative ideas with Nadine and found her new teacher to be very receptive. Within a short time their working relationship changed. Nadine became very demanding. A minor mistake was met with vicious attacks. Nadine saw Stacy as a potential rival and did everything she could to block her progress. She criticized Stacy at every opportunity. These events resulted in screaming matches. Nadine picked away at Stacy. Her voice grew louder and louder as she found greater fault with the quality of her student's work. It was not unusual for Nadine to call Stacy "ignorant" and "stupid" in the presence of others. Nadine told Stacy that she "would never be able to make it in the business," that she "simply lacked the talent and drive." Nadine's rage escalated. It bubbled over like an underground volcano, spewing to the surface in great fiery bursts.

The force of narcissistic rage is cataclysmic, designed to leave no survivors. The timing of its eruptions is unpredictable. There is no chance to escape and run for cover. The victim feels invaded, even assaulted. The aftermath causes emotional pain and devastation. The victim rises slowly and cautiously, checking himself for injuries. Expressing gratefulness for having lived through the ordeal, he anxiously wonders when the next violent jolt will occur and if he will survive it.

Rage is not anger. Anger is focused on righting wrongs and satisfying needs. Anger has a beginning and an end. When the goal is reached, the wrong adjudicated, the need satisfied, anger ceases. Long after the injustice has been rectified, the injury healed, the apology made—rage continues. Rage is primal; it is born and grows out of the core of the self. Rage promises chaos and destruction. Narcissistic rage propagates in the earliest years of childhood. It is the psychological remnant of a lack of parental empathy. Bottomless rage emerges from the severe psychological wounding of not being loved and cherished for one's true nature. The child who must forfeit his authenticity to survive is the adult filled with rage. As a childhood victim, the narcissist unconsciously cries: "You didn't love me for myself but for my gifts, my brilliance, my attractiveness. I could never be myself. You never gave me a chance. I became the child who reflected your self-importance and attempted to fulfill your ego needs. I hate you and want to destroy you."

Bottomless rage begins with self-hatred. Narcissists harbor a contempt for themselves that is projected onto all of those who share their lives—spouses, girlfriends (boyfriends), children, business partners, friends, acquaintances, even strangers. No one is spared their wrath. The recipient of narcissistic rage feels embattled. He is caught off guard by the unpredictability and force of the attack. The narcissist is capable of rapid oscillations in his attitude toward you. In a single day he can be your best friend or an archenemy. No one is prepared for his abrupt mood shifts. These individuals perpetuate an atmosphere of apprehension and anxiety. Witnessing these shifting emotional weather fronts, one feels helpless, fearful, and inadequate. Narcissistic rage is fierce and relentless. Like the flow of lava to the sea, it offers no dispensations and shows no mercy.

With rage constantly riding on the narcissist's shoulder, there are certain circumstances that produce major explosions in him. A classic case involves real or perceived betrayals by close associates and confidants. Josh, a twenty-five-year-old boy wonder, was hired by William to run one of the divisions of his elite publishing empire. Early on, William turned to Josh to both solve problems and share the creation of a new vision for the company. William gravitated toward the young man's intellect, drive, and self-confidence. In the beginning, Josh idealized his boss, viewing him as a man of considerable acumen and savvy in the publishing world. After a few years, Josh held a powerful position as co-partner and confidant to William. Although William took all the credit for their accomplishments, he depended on Josh for professional advice. Josh had become William's alter ego. Quietly and secretly, Josh used his quick rise in the company to springboard into a more challenging and prestigious professional move. When William discovered that Josh was leaving, he felt as if his arm had been amputated. How could Josh do this to him? His sense of betrayal quickly transformed into a seething rage.

He wanted to reach out and kill Josh with his bare hands. William became obsessed with revenge. His vindictiveness had no limits. He vowed to smear Josh and obstruct his meteoric career one way or another. William continues the war. He will not stop until he has mortally wounded his former partner and confidant.

Narcissistic rage is fueled by intense self-loathing. The narcissist unconsciously despises those qualities in himself that he views as dependent and weak. Rage overflows in the narcissist when:

- his image is besmirched (threat of loss of attractiveness or loss of social or financial standing)
- others view him as imperfect
- he loses absolute control
- he is forced to admit he made a mistake
- he discovers a betrayal by a loyal lieutenant
- a rival shows him up
- he is publicly humiliated

## PERNICIOUS ENVY

Envy is a secret, taboo emotion. People don't talk about their envies. Being envious makes us look bad. It is unseemly and embarrassing to openly admit that we want what someone else has. Envy is a strong, forbidden emotion, one of the seven deadly sins. There is no one more envious than a narcissist. They covet the beauty, youth, sexual prowess, and worldly power of competitors. They plot to get what they are determined to have, which belongs to someone else. Their envy is venomous.

Envy in the narcissist is skillfully hidden. Yet it burns in his gut. The narcissist conceals his envy from himself. After all, he knows he is the best. Why should he be envious of someone who is his inferior? This envy arises from a deep self-hatred. He hates those who love one another, knowing that he can never attain their state of commitment and devotion. He is confounded by human warmth, mutual dedication, and affection. Unconsciously the narcissist knows that he doesn't lead a meaningful life, that beneath it all he is a fraud.

Jason and Fred became friends in art school. In the intervening years, Jason experienced great success as a commercial artist. He opened his own gallery and was influential in the art market. Fred struggled throughout his young adulthood to hone his skills and develop as a fine artist. Monetary compensation had eluded him until later in his career. After a series of critically acclaimed one-man shows, his work took off and he began to make a great deal of money. Jason and Fred became reacquainted. On a superficial level, Jason congratulated Fred on his recent triumphs. Secretly, he was envious and hated Fred for his success and in particular for his artistic talent, which was now being recognized. Jason had always told himself that Fred was a small operator who painted solely out of personal indulgence and assumed that he would never be noticed, let alone receive critical reviews and have his paintings sell out at every show. While Jason treated Fred as if the old relationship had resumed, he did everything in his power to block the showing of Fred's work in prominent galleries. Secretly he used his contacts in the art community to undermine Fred's future efforts to display his work. Jason's envy was dark and blind, containing a malevolent quality.

## CLOSET PARANOID

The narcissist has many enemies, real and imagined. He spends a lot of time and energy planning elaborate attacks against those who would destroy him. Beneath it all, he trusts no one. He functions in an atmosphere of constant siege. He is suspicious even of his chosen few, a coterie of loyalists who are willing to fall on their swords for him.

Paranoia is a pervasive fear that others will harm or even destroy us. The narcissist lives in an unfriendly and dangerous inner world, despite the power and glamour of his external life. Inside, he is paranoid, tormented by anticipated attacks of perceived enemies. These core suspicions are the remnants of hidden, cold, aggressive internal parental images that he experiences as persecutors. All of this is concealed by the narcissist, who gives an impression of feeling secure. Dwayne, the CEO of a commercial real estate company, insists on elaborate security measures. He routinely tapes telephone conversations without permission from the other party. Dwayne listens to the tape repeatedly, dissecting every nuance of the conversation, looking for potentially incriminating information. This secret procedure is used to marginalize and destroy enemies and as ammunition for future battles. Dwayne demands that his staff call him from "safe" phones or see him in person to ensure that their conversations can't be surreptitiously overheard or traced. In addition, he works closely with a favorite investigator to obtain secret, embarrassing details of the private lives of his perceived enemies and close associates. He lives in constant fear that others will destroy him. Although he courts envy with his flamboyant lifestyle and many luxurious perks, he is fully aware that there are dangerous forces in the shadows that can annihilate him. This justifies his use of invasive, illegal tactics. Beneath these elaborate security rituals, Dwayne is deeply paranoid.

The narcissist assumes the role of saboteur as a way of fending off real and imagined enemies. He is an expert at setting others up. The dance begins with his pursuit of the prospective victim. He quickly becomes the avid listener and confidant. He meticulously collects the intimate details of his new friend's life, searching for and teasing out areas of vulnerability. He is masterful here, intuitively understanding the exact formula of personal secrets and weaknesses that will destroy his target.

Lisbeth, who after college used her drive and important contacts to work her way up the studio ladder, was in line to become an assistant director for a major film project. She found out through her sources that another woman with directorial experience, Paula, was her chief competitor for the coveted position. Lisbeth saw her rival as an archenemy and decided to do some detective work. She discovered that Paula had suffered from some past psychological problems and had been hospitalized after an attempted suicide. Lisbeth maliciously spread this personal information to all of her associates. She purposely met with Paula's supervisor, and in a feigned sympathetic tone, expressed her concern that Paula was too mentally unstable to cope with the stress of an assistant director's role. It might cause her to have another breakdown. Lisbeth's detective work paid off. She secured the position, while Paula was left without a job or an explanation. Exhilarated by her triumph, Lisbeth went about her business. When others asked if she knew what had happened to Paula, Lisbeth shrugged and said, "Poor thing—it's a mystery to me."

## INJURIES AND SLIGHTS

The narcissist expects others to mirror him perfectly. He permanently casts you in the role of yes man. When a narcissist looks into your eyes, not only does he see his reflection but he expects you, in your words, gestures, and actions, to feed back to him his flawless vision of himself. Doing less than this enrages the narcissist and causes him to feel emotionally injured. The smallest criticism or oversight is a source of wounding. The narcissist has a brittle ego that doesn't bend to the minor blows and indignities that we all must endure. Narcissistic egos are rigid, vulnerable to the subtlest slight. It is ironic that those who are so comfortable inflicting body blows on others cannot tolerate even the mildest criticism or affront. The flicker of an eyelash, a dismissive hand gesture, silence itself, can mean disapproval.

Russell, the president of a business management company, attended a dinner meeting with two prospective clients. The newest partner in the firm, Vanessa, was invited to lend support to a campaign that would attract prospective clients to the firm. Russell gave a long detailed presentation, highlighting the advantages of becoming associated with his company. Near the end of the meeting, Vanessa added a subsidiary point to the talk. Russell immediately interpreted her contribution as a criticism. He was wounded by what he perceived as a negative critique of his comments. After dinner, he attacked Vanessa for interrupting and interfering with his presentation. He threatened to fire her if this ever happened again. She hadn't followed Russell's script religiously, and now she would be punished. In reality, Vanessa's comments were necessary, since Russell had given an inaccurate impression. His overreaction was based on the emotional sting of being judged. The fact that this had occurred in public was doubly humiliating. Regardless of her superb performance as a partner, Russell will always feel sensitive to any comment that Vanessa makes. He reminds himself that he can fire her at a moment's notice and dispose of his problem. Like the princess in the story "The Princess and the Pea," the narcissist is vulnerable to the most infinitesimal criticism or slight.

## HIDDEN DESPAIR

Behind a mask of bravado, the narcissist suffers from deep despair. Unconsciously, he knows that he is a fraud. He has played roles all his life in exchange for love. He deludes himself and others into believing that these performances are real. From childhood, he mastered the parts that most pleased his audience and ensured endless applause.

There are unspoken words between the future narcissist and his mother or father. "Be what I expect of you—brilliant, confident, attractive, talented, strong—and you will be crowned with adulation and specialness; be your true self and you will be devalued and discarded." For purposes of survival, the child cast away his real feelings—sadness, fear, loss, longing, tenderness—any sign of weakness that didn't fit the narrow role dictated by his parents. But there are consequences to leading a false life. When life is performed rather than lived, it is hollow inside. The emotional residue of acting at life rather than living it is despair.

Aging for the narcissist is a special horror. As middle age winds down into old age, the meticulously erected illusions crumble. Physical attractiveness diminishes. Sexual vigor and potency decrease, fueling feelings of helplessness. It is during these crises that narcissists often turn to much younger partners as lovers, boyfriends, husbands, or wives. In some instances, men start new families with young wives to reconstitute a sense of lost potency and desirability. These are measures that appear to work. They are actually signs of desperation and disintegration.

Terence enjoyed celebrity as a director of science fiction thrillers. Although his films never reached a high artistic level, he was an icon of the genre. He began his career as a film editor and was soon directing low-budget features. He had a gift for marketing mass-produced films, one right after the other. His success was repeated many times over, and he became very wealthy. He deluded himself into believing that he was a cinematic artist. Throughout his life, Terence treated people brutally, always pushing his own agenda. All of his relationships, both personal and professional, were tainted, bearing the mark of repeated intentional cruelties. His personal life was very complex. He had been married four times and had five children (one of them by a previous mistress). Terence used up the goodwill of his wives and children, as well as his friends and business associates. All his energies and motivations over his long life were narrowly focused: there wasn't an act, opinion, feeling, or perception that wasn't self-referential. *Self* was the touchstone of his being. Nothing else mattered. At the age of seventy-five Terence enjoyed every possible material luxury. He had traveled extensively throughout the world. He had achieved great fame. But a vital piece was missing. He had won the whole world and lost his soul. Terence died alone, enraged that he had not been treated with the deference he deserved. In the end he was overwhelmed by a hopelessness that wore him down until nothing was left.

A life of illusion, selfishness, and callousness catches up with the narcissist. He has incurred countless enemies. He has injured so many. Like candy wrappers strewn along a long road, he has used people up over the years. Everyone crossing his path was disposable. Victims of his treacheries, malignant lies, and broken promises continue to suffer. He has exploited and thrown away the lives of hundreds, even thousands, of people. The fateful accumulation of ill will has tipped; the act is worn and tawdry—old age has come to call. The narcissist knows that his life is over. His despair deepens to meet death.

Ultimately, the narcissist is burdened with a cold undeveloped heart that cannot be warmed or penetrated. Calling upon his familiar role as a magnetic individual with smooth social graces, he effects a convincing pseudo-empathy. Beneath this beguiling mask, he is a merciless fraud.

# CHAPTER SIX

# *Hardened Heart:*

# *Treating Others*

# *Without Empathy*

*My heart is turned to stone; I strike it, and it hurts my hand.*

— WILLIAM SHAKESPEARE, *Othello*[1]

Without empathy we are incomplete human beings. An empathic individual has the ability to emotionally merge with and feel himself into another person's emotional state. A deep understanding of what someone else is experiencing—pain, joy, fear, desperation, despair, emptiness, rage—is the result. We can actually feel the energy of an empathic person. He takes us in with a special kind of holding. His eyes embrace us, he listens intently, *his* problems and concerns have been neatly put away. He attunes himself psychologically to our difficulties rather than his own. As the popular phrase has it, "He is there for us." True empathy springs from an open heart and a dropped ego that is able to focus deep attention and concern upon someone else.

Empathy evolves through contact with loving parental responses to the needs of a child. The child who is cherished and valued for himself learns to treat others with empathy. Empathy begins when the mother and father first hold their baby. Perhaps it starts even earlier, in the womb. Does a child know he is loved as he listens to the beating of his mother's heart within her body's walls? The way the mother caresses her child, talks to him, makes eye contact, is critical. Is she tender and warm or rough, indifferent, and cold?

The potential for empathy is born within us. Some individuals are naturally more sensitive and therefore capable of internalizing the feelings of others from the beginning. The major share of our ability to empathize begins with the relationship with the primary caregiver: mother, father, a relative, or a surrogate parent. Mother's touch, smell, tone of voice, her gaze, are permanently recorded in the consciousness of the baby, throughout his body and mind, his nervous system, organs, within the smallest cell. One of the most beautiful experiences is watching a young mother with her beloved child. Her attention is focused on him, even though she may be performing other tasks. There is a constant dialogue taking place, both spoken and unspoken, between the two parties. Their eyes meet frequently. Mother and child respond to each other in intimate ways known especially to them. The baby reaches for mother and she encloses him in her arms, encouraging him with her soft murmurings. When he is in physical or emotional distress, a mother knows how to comfort her baby. She picks him up gently, rocks him, soothes his concerns with the tone and rhythm of her voice. Mother or the primary caregiver ministers to her child during the day and at times throughout the night, repeating her behaviors of comfort and reassurance. These positive responses are internalized by the baby. He learns that when he is in need, someone will respond in a uniquely personal way. An indelible knowing develops in the baby, a feeling of fundamental security.

Decades ago, the great psychiatrist Erik Erikson beautifully described this steady psychological state: "For the first component of a healthy personality I nominate a sense of *basic trust*. . . . By 'trust' I mean what is commonly implied in reasonable trustfulness as far as others are concerned and a simple sense of trustworthiness as far as oneself is concerned."[2] With the word "basic," Erikson is stating that these qualities are not "especially conscious."[3] The baby and small child learn through all of the maternal interactions and ministrations that they are loved and cherished. This foundation slowly builds within him. Eventually this feeling of intrinsic trust will sprout seeds of empathy for others, which flower throughout his life.

The young child feels that he is the center of the universe, that all of his needs must be fulfilled at any given moment. How often have you witnessed dramatic displays of temper in public places like markets or stores, when a toddler insists he must have a particular item (candy, a toy, or some object that attracts his attention). The genuinely loving parent is capable of saying, "No, dear, you are not the center of the universe." If the bond between parent and child is strong and flexible, these power struggles will act as life lessons. The child learns that mother or father can deny him something that he wants but that they still love him.

Empathy does not mean that a mother or father doesn't correct his child when he is inconsiderate or mean. Some children have cloying parents who bombard them with endless material possessions, acceding to their every wish and demand. Rewarding a child's inappropriate behavior is not empathic. It teaches the child that he can always get his way if he is clever and manipulative.

A person never forgets the delight, disgust, rage, or indifference that his mother (or primary caretaker) felt toward him from the time of his birth to the moment of death. Children know when they are not wanted and certainly can sense if they are hated or wished dead. I have known several individuals whose mother or father actually tried to kill them on more than one occasion. Often, these victims of such cruelty and horror are unable to form any close or intimate relationships throughout their lives. They remain in a state of psychological isolation and paranoia, always taking preemptive moves to protect themselves from some imagined attack.

The conscious and especially unconscious emotions that the mother feels toward herself and her baby leave an imprint at the core of the child's being. The neurological fibers of the nervous system speak in their mysterious ways, revealing whether we were loved or unloved. The thoughts that move through our intellect reverberate with words, looks, attitudes, and emotions that were communicated to us from the beginning. How we treat others—with respect, disdain, aloofness, warmth—reflects how we have felt about ourselves since we were infants and toddlers. Most people cope by pretending that they were loved and cared for. Indeed, there are many individuals who experienced adequate mothering and who consequently feel psychologically safe, grounded, and good. Some of us spend much of our lives undoing the psychological damage of knowing that we were an inconvenience, a nuisance, a threat, an afterthought.

On the surface, the empathy of the narcissist seems to be genuine. With a mastery of social graces and his quick study of human nature, the high-level narcissistic personality appears to care about our deepest and most intimate thoughts and feelings. He uses this ability to tap into the other person's narcissistic needs for admiration, praise, recognition, and power. Behind the feigned attentiveness and apparent concern is cool calculation. Pseudo-empathy is exquisitely designed by the narcissist to manipulate others so they will fulfill *his* narcissistic needs.

Pseudo-empathy is packaged as a finely tuned performance, an act that convinces most people. The narcissist focuses all of his attention on you like a laser beam. He gives you the impression that you are not alone as long as he is by your side, solving your problems, anticipating your needs. He makes you feel good: more beautiful (handsome), confident, brighter, entitled, sexier than you could ever imagine. In the embrace of an accomplished narcissist, we can easily be deluded. We stand on the highest peak, arms spread wide, surveying all that is ours. How grandiose we can become under his irresistible spell.

The narcissist always has a variety of scenarios in mind for those caught in his web of enchantment. He wants something that each one can supply him: money, an entrée to powerful connections, a stunning woman or man at his (or her) side, an impulsive sexual embrace, a convivial drinking companion. Like any great predator—an eagle in the highest branch of a fir tree who sees all, a red-tailed hawk figure-eighting in the open sky, a cheetah stalking in the tall golden grasses—he knows whom to single out for the kill and how to fell his prey.

The high-level narcissist is gifted at radiating immense charm when he chooses. This magnetic indefinable attribute is invaluable to all human beings. Charm is an energy, a vibration, a contagious optimistic state of mind. Charm beguiles; it can seduce us to do almost anything. The expression "pouring on the charm" has a truthful ring. It is a magic elixir that sets us soaring. We feel charm's embrace in the personality vibrations of a great leader or the sexual energy of a gorgeous film star. Small babies possess charm. It arises from them like an incandescent light. When we are charmed, we are entranced. Our fears, doubts, and worries evaporate. We feel giddy as if we are taking a magnificent ride above the gravitational pull of the ordinary world. If we are completely charmed, we feel godlike: all-powerful, omniscient, immortal. Unlike the baby's, the charm of the narcissist is deliberate and studied. He is watching for your reaction to his advances and compliments. His acting mode is in full blown. He has set out to catch you in his net. Will you be able to wake up, wiggle out, and escape, or will you become another victim of his pseudo-empathy?

## AYN RAND: SELF-OBSESSED VIRTUOSO

Flamboyant philosopher and novelist of best sellers *The Fountainhead* and *Atlas Shrugged*, Ayn Rand played a compelling role as a classic supernarcissist. Grandiose, pathologically self-absorbed, cunning, vindictive, Rand built an intellectual cult of followers who worshiped at her elaborate throne. The darling of a loyal band of Northeastern and West Coast intellectuals, business leaders, academics, and college students, Rand rose to prominence during the fifties and sixties as the architect of a new philosophical system called Objectivism. Objectivism chooses the reasoning process as the sine qua non of human behavior. Irrationality and the spontaneous expressions of feelings are rejected as inferior qualities. The needs and desires of the individual reign over the benefits to the group. Actions must be driven by self-interest. In economics, capitalism and free markets have supremacy over the state.

*The Passion of Ayn Rand*, by Barbara Branden, a close friend and follower of Rand's for nineteen years, offers a chilling portrait of a woman incapable of empathy. Branden speaks of their first encounter, how she was struck by Rand's penetrating eyes and the full range of their expression: intelligent, childlike, cruel, cold, desperate, vengeful, enraged, judgmental. Branden describes what was missing, however, in all their years together, through triumph, betrayal, and tragedy: "There was something I never saw in Ayn Rand's eyes. They never held an inward look—a look of turning inside to learn one's own spirit and consciousness. They gazed only and always outward."[4]

On February 2, 1905, in St. Petersburg, Russia, Alissa Zinovievna Rosenbaum was born. Alissa would become famously known as Ayn Rand. From the beginning Alice (Alissa) had a deeply strained relationship with her mother, Anna. There was never a hint of love or true affection between them. Anna openly told her children that they were unwanted and that she took care of them out of a sense of duty alone. Mother and daughter were polar opposites. Anna was frenetically social, nonintellectual, constantly busy. Anna appreciated her serious, misanthropic daughter for her intellectual prowess and academic achievements. Alice's relationship with her father, a successful self-made chemist, was tolerable although formal and distant. They engaged in intellectual discussions when Alice reached her teens. Alice was a loner. Children at school avoided and dismissed her as odd and eccentric, and she was removed from the normal social milieu. "From her parents and from the other adults she encountered, love and admiration were purchased by the qualities of her mind."[5]

Ayn Rand grew up in a tumultuous period that witnessed the fall of the czar and the rise of the violent Bolsheviks. Forced from their comfortable environs in St. Petersburg, the Rosenbaums fled to the Crimea, where they eked out a subsistence living. Here, Rand was subjected to daily doses of hunger, cold, and fear. The childhood years under the crushing yoke of communism brought feelings of hopelessness and humiliation. It wasn't the lack of food that caused Ayn psychological pain at that time and for the rest of her life. It was the dreariness, the absence of hope, the incessant grimness of daily life—the total futility of existence itself.

Rand hid her childhood memories from others and particularly from herself. In the words of one of her powerful male characters, she defiantly sums up her attitude toward her early years: "Don't ask me about my family, my childhood, my friends or my feelings. Ask me about the things I think . . . the specific events of my private life are of no importance whatever."[6]

It is not surprising that a narcissistic core self was born within the psyche of Alice Rosenbaum. She was never accepted for her authentic self: the little girl who felt so alone, overwhelmed by unacknowledged and unexpressed feelings of fear, humiliation, vulnerability, dependence, anger, desperation. Mother openly disliked her daughter, thinking of Alice as a burden. Both parents fixated on the value of her intellect alone. She was the brains of the family, the brilliant student of the academy. To be true to herself, Alice would have had to come to terms with her childhood emotional pain. This was impossible. Worshiped by her parents and others for her intelligence alone, Alice unconsciously fashioned a grandiose false self as a defensive psychological survival mechanism.

*Freeing Yourself from the Narcissist in Your Life*

At age twenty-one, after college, Alice Rosenbaum obtained a visa and moved to Chicago to live with her aunts. Shortly after her arrival in the United States, Alice gave herself a new name. She chose Ayn, the name of a Finnish writer. She picked Rand when she looked down at her Remington-Rand typewriter. She knew this sounded right. Ayn's stay with her Jewish relatives in Chicago was very mixed. They were a warm, religiously observant family. Ayn felt awkward and alone in the heart of such a close, caring group. Her visit with them was difficult because of her penchant for self-absorption and her complete lack of awareness and consideration for the feelings of others. Ayn moved to Hollywood, surviving in low-level jobs that she despised. It was during this time that Ayn met Frank O'Connor on the set of D. W. Griffith's *King of Kings*—she as an extra, he as a bit player. They were attracted to each other quickly. Ayn always claimed that she was deeply in love with Frank. He was fond of Ayn and in awe of her intelligence. Their friends always wondered if their marriage was motivated by Ayn's problematic immigration status. She would soon have to return to Russia. Marriage to Frank would solve this problem; Ayn was determined to stay in the United States. It would have not been out of character for Frank, kind and self-sacrificing, to be gallant, rescuing her by forming a marital union. After some work in the Hollywood studios, Ayn published *The Fountainhead*, her second novel, fated for great success.

During the period when she was writing her most ambitious novel, *Atlas Shrugged*, Ayn met a young couple, Barbara Weidman and Nathaniel Branden. A few years later Ayn and Frank celebrated their wedding. The Brandens became the center of a worshipful circle surrounding Ayn Rand, named the Collective. Several years into the philosophical movement, it became very obvious that Ayn and Nathaniel, a psychology student twenty-five years her junior, were sexually attracted to each other. As the liaison progressed, Ayn called a meeting with Frank and her two "dear friends," Nathaniel and Barbara. Without emotion or fanfare, Ayn flatly announced that she and Nathaniel would meet one afternoon and one evening alone every week, no exceptions. After a short while she decided that their union would be total—sexually, intellectually, romantically. She assured all of the parties that the two marriages would not be disrupted, that the bond between her and Nathan was necessary and inviolate. Ayn insisted that there was one rule that could not be breached: the arrangement between her and Nathaniel must be kept secret forever. Ayn calmly explained that the length of the affair would be conditional, a year or a bit longer, nothing more. She placated the spouses: "If Nathan and I were the same age, it would be different. . . . An affair between us can only be temporary."[7] As if struck by a hypnotic trance, Barbara and Frank capitulated to Ayn's demands. Obsessed with her passion for Nathaniel and her psychological fusion with him, Ayn rescinded her promise of a short affair and insisted that the romantic and sexual arrangement be permanent. She needed and deserved no less than full possession of her youthful heroic lover.

Ayn imposed her will on the three other individuals involved in the intimate arrangements. She offered them no alternatives. Ayn, a middle-aged woman, in choosing Nathaniel as her young lover was acting out the fantasies she had conceived and given life to through the characters in her novels. Each party to the secret liaison was devastated in his own way. Frank acquiesced quietly to the arrangement, greeting Nathaniel twice a week at his door and leaving his own home while this youthful, handsome, virile man made love to his wife. Frank kept his pain to himself. He headed to the only destination that would give him temporary respite, a bar. There he distracted himself with liquor and convivial companions in a repeated destructive pattern that led him down the road to intractable alcoholism, which destroyed his health and killed his spirit.

Barbara suffered years of paralyzing panic attacks as a result of Ayn's cruel selfishness. These horrific episodes generalized throughout her life and caused intolerable distress, terror, limitations, and feelings of grave uncertainty. In response to Barbara's psychological pain, Ayn wrote a paper on the subject of Barbara's excessive emotional reactions. Ayn reached a new level of cruelty on a day when she and Nathaniel were together. Out of sheer rising intractable terror, Barbara called and asked if she could speak with Ayn and Nathan in person. In response to Barbara's desperate plea, Ayn snapped: "How *dare* you invade my time with Nathan? . . . Are you indifferent to my context? . . . No one ever helped *me* when I needed it!"[8]

Although Nathaniel was a less innocent member of the famous quartet, an enthusiastic participant in the affair whose ego soared in its wake, Ayn frequently upbraided him for not treating her with the ardor she demanded. Their student-mentor, lover-adversary relationship spanned a period of eighteen years. During all of their time together, Ayn constantly analyzed Nathaniel's psychological blocks and deficiencies. Her reckless skewering spared no one. Nathaniel sums up the startling lack of compassion in Ayn's fateful romantic obsession: "As to Barbara's feelings, I doubt if Ayn seriously considered them. She wanted me to override two marriages, the age difference and every kind of conventional objection—and I did so."[9]

During meetings of the Collective, Ayn would launch into open-attack mode if she was philosophically challenged. Her assaults were brutal and relentless. She laid bare the private psychological world of her humiliated helpless victims. On one occasion, she let Nathaniel perform the dirty deed. Barbara Branden observes: "That evening, Ayn exhibited a lack of human empathy that was astonishing." As Nathaniel pointed out a young woman's character defects, Ayn's reaction was predictable. "Each time, Ayn chuckled with appreciation—and clapped her hands in applause."[10]

Ayn Rand, the self-appointed priestess of morality and reason, conducted her professional and personal life often without access to these qualities herself. Explosive, venomous, sadistic, Ayn tore into her intimates and cult followers like a male lion chomping on a fresh kill. While she preached reason, her god, Ayn acted out her fantasies impulsively and recklessly without the slightest regard to the harm it was causing others. Ayn accepted only blind obedience. Those who questioned her philosophical tenets were instantly lambasted and humbled. She was incapable of admitting mistakes. Ayn's narcissistic lack of empathy and her reflexive ability to blame held steely firm: "The fantasy self-image of perfection that she had spent a lifetime constructing was not to be toppled. The destruction of her relationship with Nathaniel could only be *his* fault, *his* evasions, *his* guilt."[11]

The last scenes in the Ayn Rand opera were melodramatic and unseemly. When Ayn discovered that Nathaniel had secretly been having an affair with Patrecia Gullison, a young member of the Nathaniel Branden Institute, and had withheld this information from her, Ayn turned vengeful and physically violent. In one ugly exchange, she lambasted Nathaniel and slapped him with an open hand. During an endless harangue, Ayn screamed: "Your whole act is finished! I created you, and I'll destroy you," and "You would have been nothing without me, and you will be nothing when I'm done with you!"[12] Ayn wrote an open letter to all the members who received the Objectivist newsletter describing Nathaniel's moral decrepitude. She directly stated that she had forever ended her alliance with Barbara and Nathaniel Branden and insisted that she was entitled to take back all of Nathaniel's interest in the magazine. The relationship between Ayn and Nathaniel and Barbara was irrevocably severed.

Ayn Rand's fame as a novelist and philosopher continued to grow; her novels sold with momentum and promise. For many, the philosophy and mind-set of the characters achieved biblical significance. In stark contrast, the last years of Rand's life were filled with emotional emptiness. Her husband, Frank, died, leaving her without the consummate adoring partner willing to sacrifice his life for her. Her health steadily declined despite successful lung surgery. Her heart was severely weakened, the ravages of arteriosclerosis.

As if by design, Ayn successively alienated her most loyal friends. Her demeanor with old associates who had defended and stood by her became brittle and acrimonious. She demanded that others believe exactly as she. Those who fraternized with anyone outside of her exclusive circle were ousted and vilified. Ayn's misanthropic isolation deepened. She spent hours playing solo Scrabble. One fateful morning in March 1982, Alissa Zinovevna Rosenbaum, creator of the *great* Ayn Rand, was dead. Next to her open casket stood a six-foot-high dollar sign, a quintessential personal symbol. She was quiet now, all alone. She had neither loved nor been loved. She died as she had lived, the ultimate narcissist, incapable of compassion or empathy.

## THE HEART'S CORE

The heart possesses a special intelligence. It contains within it every life experience of our existence—each sense impression, thought, terror, abandonment, joy, rage, resentment, secret. On an emotional and psychological level, when we open our hearts, we become more complete human beings. As much as we can learn with our intellects, the heart knows more.

Hatha yoga, created and developed in India over thousands of years, uses a series of specific body poses to heal the body, mend the mind, and awaken the soul. Many of these postures, combined with concentrated breathing, are designed to open heart energy that expands inner awareness and promotes health.

For millennia, Indian yogis and holy men strove for a deeper method of expanding consciousness. Among their pursuits was a system that would integrate and heal the body, mind, psyche, and soul. In the course of their search, they discovered dynamic energy centers (called *chakra*s in Sanskrit). According to the yogic system, healing takes place when energy centers are unblocked, through the use of breathing techniques and specific body positions or postures. Tensions in the body are released and energy flows more freely throughout all the systems of the body. When the body is at peace, the mind and the emotions are steady and calm. Many yoga students report that another gift of this practice is a greater awareness of their capacity for giving and receiving compassion.

Some time ago I visited a monastic on the celebration of his eightieth birthday. A small crowd gathered outdoors in a green valley amidst lacy trees, flowering shrubs, and singing birds. On first meeting Brother, I was struck by the exquisite blend of his spontaneous joy and kindness. His humility and startling realness were palpable. As he spoke to each one of us that day, his gaze was direct and personal. No trace of fear or ego could be felt coming from him. Brother was in perfect attunement with each person there, as if he had known us all of our lives. A subtle, powerful energy vibrated from him, like a flower shining in full sunlight. His heart brimmed naturally with overflowing love, simplicity, sweetness, and great humor.

The narcissist is emotionally blocked and cold, like the deepest recesses of a long-deserted tomb. Life's warm persistent breath has no residence here. No birdsong or soothing wind enters this frozen emptiness. Psychologically, the heart of the narcissist is constricted, numb, and inert. It does not move to the rhythm of life; it cannot celebrate with a full-blown laugh, a twinkling wide smile. It is untouched and untouchable, incapable of real tears of sorrow, joy, or forgiveness. This heart is unmoved when others, even close relatives and friends, are struck by serious illness or tragic life circumstances. Those who ask for mercy from the narcissist are left at the doorstep, abandoned. He can offer all the polite socially acceptable utterances, but when the moment of desperation arrives, the narcissist has vanished. The suffering of others does not stir him. He may give to charities, but this is often conditional, dependent on great fanfare and public exposure that applauds his generosity and goodness. One on one with life-and-death issues, the narcissist fails, falters, runs. Being human is an estrangement.

## CONSCIOUS SUFFERING AWAKENS EMPATHY

The Buddha told us on many occasions that the essential reality of human existence is suffering. The cycle of life beginning with birth takes a natural course from early childhood, to the verdant freshness of youth and adolescence, through the bright dreams of adulthood, into prime middle age, to a slowing drumbeat in old age, and finally death. Dealing with these inevitabilities alone causes each of us to suffer as we visualize and later experience the ultimate dissolution of body and mind. Part of handling these human verities is the recognition that the true nature of reality is impermanence. In our lives, one way or another, we must come to terms with these truths in order to ever attain any form of inner peace.

Innocent children suffer from the effects of intergenerational abuse, coldness, psychological instability, emotional indifference. In some instances, a pernicious pattern of cruelty and neglect crystallizes and becomes the legacy of parent to child over many generations. Some children simply do not survive; they are the victims of too much hatred, neglect, and abuse. At an early age, they die under the weight of their pain by means of an "accident," physical illness, or suicide.

Each person finds a unique way to deal with his suffering. Most deny it, defend against it, or project it onto others. They believe the family fairy tale that they came from a good home with normal parents, or at least tolerable ones. Nothing went terribly wrong that they can remember. These individuals stick with their life's working script. Most people, unless they are forced by extreme crises or tragedy, become defensive and angry at the implication that their childhoods were less than idyllic. Some of us cling to the happy family story despite profound life reverses. It is simply too painful to acknowledge the truth. For some, it is secreted and hidden away in a reservoir of repressed memory.

No matter how empathic our parents have been, we *all* carry some remnants of deprivation, trauma, and loss. Some children, as a result of a difficult genetic endowment or congenital circumstances of birth, have greater needs than can be fulfilled, despite their parents' best efforts. Beneath the surface of a cheery, politically correct family history, a chronic emotional numbing grows, like a wayward virus. Through psychological anesthesia, we block pain and access to our deepest feelings. We become incapable of experiencing great suffering, great joy, or great love.

I have noticed that many people are always "fine." They respond to you in dry, banal generalities. "My job is great, the kids are doing well in school." "We're in the middle of a remodel that's taking up a lot of our time." "Our teenage girls are 'good kids'" (translation: they're not rebelling). These individuals behave in a predictable choreographed manner. Their psychological barricades of long standing are fully reinforced. If *you* are "not great," "not fine," or even worse in "dreadful shape, quietly or unquietly falling apart," it makes them squirm psychologically. While sucking in impatient breaths, they pretend to listen, maintaining a tight politeness. After a few moments they hurriedly mutter an excuse: "I must get back to my project," "I have to walk the dogs," "I have errands to do," "I have a meeting." Some wordlessly turn on their heels while you are mid-sentence in explaining that you are "not fine." Your "unfineness" makes them feel so ill at ease and embarrassed that they must remove themselves from this melodramatic, over-the-top spectacle. They are so numb that their sole reaction is one of acute avoidance and annoyance, often seasoned with ragged edges of disgust.

Many use escape mechanisms to quell their suffering. They drink too much, take drugs, gamble, act out sexually, work compulsively. Working too hard has become one of modern life's greatest virtues. Our society places more value on time and productivity in a career than the personal parental care of children. Conveniently, we have nannies, babysitters, and the technological viewing of the child while he is at day care and we are at work.

When an individual drinks regularly and becomes high or drunk, he is escaping from his pain. Numbing one's pain with an alcoholic chaser appears to work. What a fix! It feels so warm, so good, so right. However, the pain reappears and he must drink again to get relief. The cycle of drinking is unending, as is the suffering. Escapes are always transitory. They delude us into believing that our suffering has evaporated and will not return like a recurring nightmare. The moment we feel the liquor working its sensual blurry way into our system, we believe the wish-fulfilling dream that the pain has ceased to exist.

Suffering is transformed by following it to its source, by visiting the truth of our life experience. The core wounds—of not being wanted, lovable, or loved, of being thrown away, discarded, or abused—must be reexperienced through a conscious process. Wounds need to be emotionally felt, not just intellectually acknowledged. This can be achieved through the psychotherapeutic process, working with a gifted professional. Careful in-depth research to find the right therapeutic fit is worthwhile.

Many therapists are so dysfunctional and inept themselves that they are unable to uncover and deal with their own psychological issues let alone those of their clients. There are psychotherapists who offer treatment only to clients who can afford their exorbitant fees. When a therapist I was seeing (highly trained and psychologically savvy) continued to raise his hourly fee, I suggested that he would soon be treating only the wealthy. Had his professional focus become skewed in a monetary direction despite his gifts as a therapist?

A therapist who has worked through his own core psychological issues and is capable of true empathy can assist his patients in uncovering and healing their hidden psychic pain. Good psychotherapy (which is rare) can help to resolve primary childhood issues, but the experience of healing stretches out beyond the horizon. It is multilayered, lifelong. We are never finished products but growing, dynamic individuals.

When we learn to live and appreciate our own truth, we become more merciful toward others and therefore capable of deep empathy. Most people resist moving through psychological pain. The earliest childhood wounds are the deepest. They occur when we are the most vulnerable and helpless. A little child of three who is terrorized by physical threats and psychological torture and beaten regularly sustains enormous damage. Some children, because of their genetic endowment, position in the family, temperament, disposition and level of sensitivity, are more resilient under severe stress, abuse, or neglect. Some therapists call these children invulnerable. No one is invulnerable. Even the strongest and most emotionally adaptable child pays a price for the inflicted abuse or careless neglect he endures.

Individuals who appear the most "normal" are often concealing depths of despair, emptiness, and rage. The externals—achievement in the world, monetary success, ambition, drive, outward appearance, social skills—are often very deceptive. We need not look very far to view huge psychological fissures appearing from the central core of the personality. The suffering is there. It can be seen in the deadened eyes that emit no light, the hollow monotone of the voice, the rigid posture, the frozen affect. Bringing pain out of the deep freeze, thawing it through purposeful awareness, and working through the thorniest psychological childhood issues bears the best fruit of all—becoming fully human.

## SOFTENING THE RESISTANT HEART

Another route toward developing empathy is through a spiritual path (in the form that it takes for each individual). The spiritual route is not quick, easy, or smooth. Some are forced in this direction as a result of some overwhelming trauma or an accumulation of lifelong suffering that can no longer be tolerated. We want to die, even kill ourselves. We have tried everything else: addictive behaviors, sexual acting out, intellectualization, numerous marriages, excessive spending, burying ourselves in a series of careers. Excellent psychotherapy does not cure all psychic ills. It can take us to a point of psychological insight and emotional working through. Psychotherapy can be exceedingly valuable. Therapy alone has limitations.

Life is a dynamic event. Like a great river, it crests, swerves, and meanders in cadence with the features of the terrain it embodies, the winds that blow, the sun and moon that rise and set upon it, the fish that swim in its waters, the seasons that define its force and shape. Spiritual waters are without boundaries. The spiritual connection is personal, constant, and present. There are no horizons here, only the deepest blue. For some, eternity is a beatific future; for others, it vibrates brightly in this moment.

Following a spiritual path is often discouraging, humbling, tedious, boring, mystifying. It requires that we acknowledge our shortcomings and failures without defensiveness. It asks us to become naked to ourselves and eventually transparent. A person who possesses the spiritual quality of transparency is always the same, despite the people or circumstances that he encounters. He moves through life with calmness, grace, and equanimity. He treats everyone with respect and lifts the psychic weight off others. His heart is strong and soft, resolute and adaptable.

Rosalie, a forty-nine-year-old book researcher, was a well-educated woman. As a child, she was expected to control her emotions above all else. Her mother, Cleo, was a cold, demanding woman. Nothing—not even perfection—was good enough for her. Rosalie's father, Raymond, was a different sort, a dreamer, almost a child himself. A public servant at work, Raymond played the role of servile child to his wife. Cleo ran the family enterprise like a warrior. Rosalie's brothers and sisters called their mother the Little General behind her back. As the oldest daughter, Rosalie was expected to take over the maternal functions that Cleo was either unwilling or unable to fulfill. Cleo worked two jobs, preferring this arrangement to staying home with a bunch of kids. By the age of three, Rosalie had become so adept at keeping her emotions under complete control that she simply felt numb.

With her fine linear brain, Rosalie earned two master's degrees: one in business, the other in English literature. She worked as a researcher for a prominent nonfiction writer. Rosalie met Mark in graduate school. After a short courtship, they were married. Within two and a half years they had two daughters, a toddler and an infant. It was very difficult for Rosalie to display a lot of warmth toward her children. As soon as each child was three months old, she returned to her career. Her work as researcher filled her with a keen sense of accomplishment. She went through the motions of her married life, often ignoring Mark. She gave most of herself to her work.

Rosalie and Mark had been married for twenty-five years, and their children were away at college. One evening, Mark told Rosalie that he wanted a divorce. His rationale was that the children were practically grown and that he needed warmth and attention in his life. Rosalie was nonplussed by this sudden announcement. It was as if a bomb had been dropped on her head. For weeks she couldn't believe that Mark was leaving her. Was he joking? Just going through a phase? Could she possibly get him to change his mind? What would happen to her without him? On very short notice, Mark moved out of the house and retained an attorney. Rosalie was forced to seek legal counsel, despite her state of shock. After much acrimony, the settlement was completed.

Six months after the divorce, Rosalie discovered that she had an aggressively growing lymphoma just below her abdomen. Surgery and chemotherapy were recommended, and Rosalie followed the course of treatment. During these long months she began to break down emotionally. Uncharacteristically, she cried constantly and experienced feelings of overwhelming loss and regret. She had a small circle of friends who assisted her through the surgery and chemo and provided emotional support. Feeling that she had hit rock bottom and no longer wanted to live, Rosalie sought the help of a professional therapist. Through intensive psychotherapy, she began to experience emotions that she had never acknowledged in her entire life: helplessness, rage, fear, shame, unworthiness, dark despair. At times she was terrorized that the medical regimen would not work and she would die. On other occasions, she longed for death and a quick reprieve from what felt to her like an impossible situation.

Rosalie began to thaw emotionally for the first time in her life. Faced with death, she was finally able to acknowledge the psychic pain that she had endured as a child, to reexperience it and to mourn the deprivations she had suffered. Rosalie reached out to a spiritual community and began a daily routine of meditation and prayer. She received great comfort and valuable insights as a result of her spiritual practice.

As time passed and her cancer receded, Rosalie emerged as a new person, someone whom she would not have recognized in the past. Now she could express her emotions without fear or shame. She began to experience love for others, particularly her children. Out of these life-and-death circumstances, Rosalie was reborn.

# PART THREE

## *The Adoring*

## *Audience*

# CHAPTER SEVEN

# The Charmed Circle:

# Worshipping at the Source

*As Wright liked to boast, they [his apprentices] were the*
*fingers on his hand, and for them it was . . . a way of life: for*
*as long as Wright was alive they would be judged as*
*appendages of a great man and not as individuals.*

— BRENDAN GILL,
*Many Masks: A Life of Frank Lloyd Wright*[1]

The narcissist draws a magical, golden circle around himself. He convinces his followers that this space is a secret garden or hidden glen. There is enchantment here. Anything is possible. Rules and restrictions that operate in the rest of the world don't apply. Those inside this chosen enclave are privileged. They breathe the air and walk in the footsteps of a great man (or woman). Members of this elite group believe that the light that shines so brightly upon the narcissist will reflect back onto them, warming each one with an incandescent glow. Those who sit at the feet of the narcissist make him the focus of their lives. He is center and source, their raison d'être. The narcissist carefully selects those who will furnish him with a consistent flow of veneration, praise, and service. The narcissist and his adoring audience are as intertwined as a sea creature and its shell.

Power, wealth, personal and professional stature—these are the enticements the narcissist uses to catch the small fish who will become members of his coterie. An astute operator, he understands the ego needs of followers: to be exclusive, to be materially comfortable, to be just like him. Although the narcissist has no insight into his own psychological processes, he is talented at identifying the secret cravings of those who press around him. His offers are tempting, frequently irresistible. Disciples of the narcissist are entranced by his capacity to have whatever he wants: material possessions, unlimited access, the deference of loyal devotees. He taps into the infantile, demanding child inside of us that wants it all. He looks into our eyes, strokes us with his enormous charisma, and promises to fulfill our secret yearnings.

## FRANK LLOYD WRIGHT:
### HIS ENCHANTED FOLLOWERS

Frank Lloyd Wright, architect and icon, attracted circles of followers and worshipers all his life. To this day, there are still believers prostrate at his throne, waiting to kiss his ring. Talented, driven, classically narcissistic—Wright always climbed to a new height, captivating many with an energy and magnetism he turned on and off like a well-designed faucet.

One of the many ways that Wright perpetuated his elaborate charmed circle was through the Taliesin Fellowship. He invited apprentices in architecture and the arts to work with him at Taliesin North and Taliesin West. In exchange for a hefty tuition, they were put to work. These young hopefuls believed they would be assisting the Great Architect on some historic endeavor. Instead, they were subjected to long hard labor, acting as low-paid servants (from draftsman to field hand) to Wright's role as "grandee: riding horseback, driving fast cars, entertaining international notables."[2] Wright was blatantly unpredictable in his payment of the apprentices. Sometimes, he asked to borrow money from them. The invention of the Fellowship was a clever way of financing his dream as well as enlarging his clique. In all the years that the Fellowship was active, very few of his apprentices achieved any independent professional acclaim. Wright always took the credit for himself, despite their arduous work or creative contributions.

Although he had a late start with females (he was a virgin when he married his first wife, Catherine), Wright had many women literally and figuratively sitting at his feet. His first marriage, to Catherine, was not exactly a love match or a soul mate found but a practical union that suited the two of them at the time. Catherine bore six children in quick succession. Throughout their marriage, Wright's curious and lustful eyes restlessly strayed. It didn't take him long to jump into a melodramatic scandal with the wife of a client and neighbor for whom he was designing a home. Wright and Mamah (Martha) Borthwick Cheney began a torrid affair. Mamah adored Wright; she was willing to give up her husband, children, and reputation for him. The liaison led to Wright's abandonment of his six children and a penniless wife. He rode the winds of his passions to the continent, where he lived idyllically with his mistress. Wright returned to his injured family after two years. Tragically, Mamah died at Taliesin in a fire deliberately set by a deranged member of the Wright family staff.

In an unfortunate life choice, Wright first took as a mistress and then married Miriam Noel, a sculptress in her forties. Temperamentally unsuited to each other, these two battled it out psychologically and even physically during most of their marriage. The union proved disastrous. Miriam was histrionic and hopelessly paranoid. She frequently threw tantrums, accusing Wright of having affairs. At times, Miriam would enact the role of adoring follower to Wright. She generously financed some of his architectural projects. Early on, Miriam displayed serious symptoms of mental illness. She descended and ascended in and out of madness.

As the marriage to Miriam deteriorated, Wright became involved in a consuming love affair with the very young, statuesque, dark-haired Olga Ivanovna Milanov Hinzenberg (called Olgivanna). She was thirty-seven years younger than he, and he was beguiled by her from their initial meeting at an evening ballet. Montenegran-born Olgivanna spent her early life in Russia and Turkey. After her first marriage failed, she moved to Fontaine-bleau, France, to immerse herself in the teachings of the philosopher Georgi Gurdjieff, part mystic, part rapscallion. Olgivanna became a loyal follower of his cult. In Olgivanna, Wright had found the truest believer within the charmed circle. This wife always had time for Frank; she was adroit at both mothering and manipulating him. Olgivanna would wrench herself from a sick-bed to participate in some activity initiated by Wright. "Wifely devotion and identification with the beloved can go no further. She had found her new reason for being."[3]

A revealing visual tableau illustrates Olgivanna as Wright's chief worshiper. A photograph in profile taken early in their marriage shows the two of them with identical hairstyles and hats positioned at an angle that gives them the appearance of twins. Wright and Olgivanna gaze in tandem with impeccable symmetry, the couple of the hour, precious bookends.

The Wright cult, nurtured throughout his life, gained even greater momentum after his death through its perpetuation by the worshipful Olgivanna. She brought the same obsessiveness and fervor to this role as she had demonstrated toward her mentor Gurdjieff. The holy rituals of Taliesin continued, as if Wright was still alive. Brendan Gill, a brilliant Wright biographer and friend, describes Olgivanna nearing the end of her life: "She had served as the priestess of a shrine whose god had gained in puissance over the years; now she was failing . . . but the god remained."[4]

## THE POWER LURE

A unique energy, not unlike sexual energy, surrounds the mighty. When a powerful man or woman enters a room, the seas part. Everyone quiets to hear his words, to observe his next move. Many are transfixed by his presence alone. Associating with a person who wields power can be intoxicating, like taking a strong drink or drug, or feeling the persistent pull of a compelling sexual attraction. Powerful people are treated differently. They are royalty, gratuitously rewarded with a largesse of undeserved respect.

High-level narcissists appear to have neither limits nor fears. A prospective follower feels secure under the wing of the narcissist and believes that some of his magic fairy dust will rub off on him. A master of control, the narcissist convinces those around him that they are safe only with him. Many followers mistakenly believe that these relationships will wipe away childhood feelings of shame and helplessness. Psychologically, they are dependent, obedient children who have never become responsible for their own lives. Tragically, they fail to activate their individual personalities and, as a result, their unique gifts and talents. They squander the hours of their lives in exquisite captivity, paying homage to their narcissistic master.

Many of the wealthy belong to a special club; they lead privileged, comfortable lives, securely removed from the common travails of everyday life—money worries, boring jobs, limited leisure. *Certainly, there are wealthy individuals who are not narcissistic, and all narcissists are not wealthy.* However, some narcissists use the pursuit of wealth to perpetuate their imposing self-images. The material blessings that flow from wealth and set these individuals apart appeal to the narcissist's grandiloquent view of himself.

Members of the golden circle are lured not only to the magnetic charm of the narcissist but to the protective shield of his wealth. Pampered in the warm glow of plenty, they vicariously share his feelings of entitlement. Misguided and deluded, they are soothed by the perks and possessions bestowed on them by their leader. Beneath the shiny seduction of this sycophantic role lie feelings of worthlessness and self-hatred.

The narcissist is inevitably preoccupied with the impression he is making. More than the quality of his character, it is how others perceive him that matters most. High-level narcissists tend to spend a lot of money on themselves. They demand the very best. Everything in their environment—homes, cars, personal appearance, clothing—must reflect a flawless persona. Walking through some of their homes, one wonders if anyone lives there. There is no sign of human habitation: no footprints on rugs or carpets, no finger marks on furniture or mirrors, no body or cooking aromas, no whiffs of faded perfume, no towel askew, no cushion indentations, no stain, no dust, no scuff, no smudge. Every aspect of their outward surroundings—personal possessions, clothing, homes, cars, planes—is kept in pristine condition at all times. I have known narcissists who purchased new cars so frequently that they didn't wait to obtain license plates let alone allow ashtrays to become half full.

The narcissist's devotees ensure that his world is always in a state of absolute order. They expend great amounts of time and energy focusing on the details and minutiae of his life. Germaine had worked for Richard for fifteen years as a housemaid. She had been trained in Europe and was employed by some of the finest hotels. After his wife died, Richard married Germaine. He was physically attracted to her and knew that she would be fully subservient to him. Under Germaine's supervision their home was meticulously maintained. You could go over every millimeter of the house with a microscope and not find a hair, the tiniest insect corpse, a speck of errant dust, even a water mark. Richard's suits were hung exactly three inches apart in his many closets. His shoes were precisely catalogued; each dress shirt was coffined in a custom-designed drawer. Richard's demands for cleanliness and order were pathological. If the smallest mistake was made, Germaine was singled out for violent verbal abuse. Openly weeping and almost hysterical on these occasions, Germaine shook with fear and humiliation. She felt desperate to leave but reminded herself that she belonged with Richard in this magnificent home. She had long ago relinquished her freedom and dignity. Germaine had come to accept Richard as a cruel minder. The bargain that she struck was worth her life. In exchange for her subservience, Germaine would be protected by Richard's financial security.

## IRRESISTIBLE LIFESTYLES

Members of the charmed circle are seduced by the lifestyle they share with the narcissist. There are the multiple homes and fine furnishings, countless first-class international trips, associations with prominent individuals, memberships in exclusive country clubs, invitations to the fashionable parties, the best tables at haute cuisine restaurants. These are the perks offered to prospective followers. Spouses, mistresses, and lovers are easily lured by the glitzy paraphernalia of an opulent lifestyle. Being endlessly coddled is its own aphrodisiac.

Intimates of the narcissist pay a high price for their loyalty. They weather psychological and at times physical abuse, countless extramarital affairs, illegitimate children, even sexually transmitted diseases, to be counted among the blessed. Like worshipers clinging to a profligate guru, they hitch their fate and future to the privileges and comforts they were falsely promised. Like parasitic fish that fuse with and clean the leviathans of the sea, devotees are inextricably attached to their master.

Katlin, a thirty-three-year-old divorcée, met Thomas, a seventy-six-year-old media mogul. After a brief dating period, Katlin and Thomas were married. With unlimited time and financial resources at his disposal, Thomas was accustomed to a life of profligate indulgence. Katlin shared the benefits of this lifestyle. In exchange for the luxury travel and fine homes, she had to deal with Thomas's compulsive sexual behaviors. Katlin begged him to go into therapy with her to save their marriage. He refused. She threatened to leave him if he didn't change. Each time Katlin capitulated. She told herself that she truly loved Thomas and would remain loyal to him. She convinced herself that they were soul mates.

During one particularly ignominious cycle, Thomas spent a number of weeks conducting negotiations with a business partner and friend in Europe. Upon his return, after lengthy interrogations and, finally, a "confession," Katlin discovered that both men had spent much of their time engaging in high-risk sexual liaisons with call girls and street prostitutes. Katlin was so confused and distraught by these revelations that she wept in public and related this sordid tale to friends and acquaintances. Katlin swore that this was the end, the last humiliation. She exploded at Thomas over the dangers of her contracting sexually transmitted diseases as a result of his impulsive sexual forays. She knocked on neighbors' doors day and night, crying and ranting hysterically to anyone present that she was a victim of a persecutory, philandering husband. She repeated all the details of his sexual transgressions to strangers. She fumed, telling her neighbors and friends how much she detested him. Katlin let everyone know that she was hiring the most aggressive lawyer she could find to obtain an immediate divorce.

Several weeks after this drama unfolded, and to everyone's astonishment, Katlin brightly announced that she and Thomas, accompanied by a group of their intimate friends, would be leaving for a two-month African safari. Katlin stressed that this event was particularly meaningful to her since it would take place on their wedding anniversary. She planned to have their vows renewed in Africa. How could Katlin make such a swift turnabout in the aftermath of her husband's monumental acts of betrayal and endangerment? Everyone was flabbergasted. The not-so-mysterious reason Katlin would endure the humiliating cycles of abuse and never leave Thomas was her fear of losing her opulent lifestyle. Without the sparkling "Thomas package," she felt worthless; alone she was nothing. Katlin would bear all the humiliation and shame of her husband's multiple infidelities, even the possibility of contracting a sexually transmitted disease in exchange for a privileged life. Thomas knew that Katlin would stay with him, despite any impulse he chose to gratify. Katlin remained on board; being Thomas's wife wasn't so bad after all.

## SUPPORTING ACTORS,
## BIT PLAYERS, AND EXTRAS

Life with a narcissist is neither simple nor straightforward. It is a complex production that requires the right settings, scripts, and actors. The narcissist is encircled by a theatrical cast of supporting actors, bit players, and extras. Good supporting actors are invaluable. Playing their parts skillfully, they intensify the drama, drawing attention to the star. The supporting actors in "the big picture show"—spouses, mistresses, business partners—amplify the leading man's performance. Supporting actors frequently relinquish their life destinies to the narcissist. Their hearts beat in rhythm to the tempo of *his* days.

Elaine had been married to Luke, a television actor, for more than thirty years. During all this time Elaine had worked and taken care of the children while Luke established himself in the entertainment business. From the beginning, Luke's wishes and needs always came first. Although she was resentful at times, Elaine accepted Luke's self-centeredness, attributing it to a creative temperament. Elaine's feelings for Luke went beyond admiration; he was a great artist. When he was on a soundstage taping a show, Elaine sat in the dark, applauding every nuance of his performance. Over the years Luke strayed countless times; Elaine always took him back. She was ever-forgiving, overlooking his massive insensitivities and betrayals. Elaine rationalized that this was the price for being married to a successful actor. After years of living in the shadow of her narcissistic husband, Elaine remains the steadfast supporting actor, loyally deferring to the star to create her role and define her life.

A good bit player is versatile and flexible, available to the star performer at all times. Bit players are often cast in character roles. Reliable and predictable, they add spice to the story line. Though skillful in their parts, bit players rarely become stars. Highly discreet, he (or she) always finds a way to fulfill any request. Dan, a private pilot and general factotum, had worked for Austin, a software mogul, for over ten years. Dan was a jack-of-all-trades. Austin could count on him day or night to fulfill his varied missions: arranging impromptu luxury junkets, procuring attractive young women, sending flowers and gifts to wives and mistresses. When the occasion arose, Dan acted as a private investigator, searching out confidential incriminating information on Austin's enemies that could be used for intimidation purposes and subtle blackmail. This function was of particular value to Austin. He was able to get the "dirt" he needed through Dan without leaving a trace of his direct involvement. Dan was a fixture in Austin's life, a polished loyal bit player.

Extras on movie sets are expendable; one is interchangeable with another. Extras are hired for their physical presence; they are not chosen for their talents, personalities, or general appeal. Like wildebeests stampeding through the bush, they are part of the herd. Lumped into a whole, they are often called the atmosphere. Extras move in and out of the narcissist's world as needed or by whim. They are stage-door groupies and hangers-on. Narcissists often travel with entourages depending on how powerful and famous they are. Some extras are so enamored of the narcissist that they are willing to act in any number of roles. They will fetch and carry, have a one-night stand, endure emotional and physical abuse, do anything to remain part of the golden circle. Sheila, a massage therapist, met Robb, a film producer, when he visited a weekend spa. Sheila was taken with Robb; she had watched every film that he had produced. Sheila felt honored to work for Robb and made an effort to meet with him whenever possible. After a very brief acquaintance, Sheila and Robb became intimate. The sexual encounter with Robb became a high point in her life. Despite a long, acrimonious marriage, several mistresses, and many girlfriends, Robb engaged in frequent impulsive affairs that he found to be dangerously exciting. Sheila had sex with Robb whenever he called or dropped over uninvited, often in the middle of the night. She always said yes, telling herself that she was a vital part of Robb's life. Sheila is a classic extra, offering herself as a vehicle for reckless no-limits behavior.

## A PERPETUAL FOUNTAIN OF PRAISE

Like water cascading down a falls, compliments and tributes must flow to the narcissist at all times. He expects and counts on this praise as a lifeline. He recounts endless stories of his triumphs and expects others to tell him "how wonderful he is." The slightest interruption in this unguent tide is disconcerting and disturbing to the narcissist. Reactions can range from feelings of being slighted and hurt to uncontrollable rage.

Members of the golden circle are expected to provide their services at any given moment and in perpetuity. It doesn't matter to a narcissist if you are about to hop on a plane for a badly needed vacation. It is unimportant that one of your children is ill and must be taken to the doctor. A daughter's wedding, a special anniversary, even a death in the family—these events are minuscule in proportion to the narcissist's *absolute* sense of self-entitlement.

Devotees spin an elaborate web, a golden aura, around the narcissist. They fawn, they glow, they hold their breaths. Their eyes glaze as their heads tilt in his direction. Under a light or heavy trance, followers are hypnotized by the narcissistic lure. Cecilia, an advertising executive, hired Diane as her administrative assistant. Cecilia promised Diane she would eventually become a partner in the business. Competent and eager, Diane spent most of her waking hours serving Cecilia. Her boss was hopelessly demanding and explosively unpredictable. Diane quickly learned that her principal job was providing Cecilia with a fountain of recirculating compliments. Diane's loyalty was blind, unquestioned. She experienced her life through Cecilia. Like a teenage fan of a rock idol, Diane would never waiver as a founding member of Cecilia's cloying fan club.

Followers of the narcissist, especially those closest to him—spouses, mistresses, lovers, children, partners—squander their life potential. They have turned themselves over to a callous exploitive parental figure who makes all the decisions. Their mission is to obey and adore him: no questions asked.

On the surface, members of this elite club appear to be well put together: aesthetically, mentally, and psychologically. Beneath this thin, often appealing, outer layer lie intense primitive feelings of resentment, rage, and despair. Living only to please and appease an imperious narcissist, combined with mounting erosions of their individual opportunities, faithful followers eventually become hate-filled enemies.

# CHAPTER EIGHT

# The Intimate Enemy:

# Living in the Shadows

*Faithful are the wounds of a friend; but the kisses of an
enemy are deceitful.*

— PROVERBS 27:5–6[1]

## COUNTERFEIT LIVES

Those who live closely with a narcissist—wives, husbands, partners, children, in particular—are required to be false to themselves. They learned in early childhood that it was unsafe to feel
and express the full range of their emotions, even to think their
own thoughts. People who throw their destinies in with a narcissist
have never developed a real sense of self. Deep inside, they feel
inadequate and worthless. When they encounter emotion in others,
they label these individuals as characterlogically weak.

The capacity to feel deeply requires a psychological sureness
and groundedness. When a person can cry freely, laugh heartily,
or become justifiably angry, he lives fully; he embraces his humanity. He does not cringe over how others will perceive or judge

him. His emotions are clear. They pour forth with unashamed naturalness.

Unexpressed and unremembered feelings cannot be buried. They voice themselves in our thoughts, dreams, sensations, and actions, in the functions of our bodies. Many people become ill as a result of malignant embedded emotions. Disowned feelings are the raw material of future autoimmune illnesses, psychosomatic disorders, cancers, and cardiovascular disease. The body always states the truth. We can delude our minds and close our hearts, but the body reveals our secrets. The body speaks the language of grief, rage, terror, hatred, envy, guilt, resentment, loss, and abandonment. As these emotions pass through the body, they transform the major organs, the hormones, the brain, the skeletal muscular system, the central nervous system.

## SELFLESS SERVANTS

Besides jeopardizing their psychological and physical health, those who live with narcissists, particularly spouses, rob themselves of vital opportunities to develop their unique creative gifts. They set aside their talents, drives, and dreams to spend huge amounts of time and energy at the disposal of a corporate wife or husband or an obsessive entrepreneur. The corporate culture of meetings, dinners, conferences, seminars, and travel is all consuming. One may wonder if the participant himself is gaining any value from the incessant cacophony of "business speak," lethal rivalries, and the constant head butting at the center of deadly power games. For many husbands, wives, and children, who are expected to wait through the long weekends and late evenings, the recurrent pattern of making work "the priority" becomes wearying, discouraging, and exasperating.

For narcissists who stand tall on the corporate ladder, their identities are tied to their careers as if by an umbilical cord. They are blind to the emotional harm they perpetrate in their eternal search for greater power and acclamation. When challenged, they intone ready excuses: "I'm the only one who knows how to handle this." "I'm doing it for my family." Or they utter the very familiar "I'm indispensable."

For hundreds of years in England, those who worked for the aristocracy in their mansions and country homes dedicated themselves to a life of service, which at that time was considered to be part of a noble tradition. Servants, born of a lower class, were destined to spend their days attending to individuals who, as a result of birth alone, owned large properties and assets. The servants were simply possessions who could be held for a length of time or simply disposed of. They led dreary, predictable lives, unable to earn enough money to become financially independent and therefore personally free. The sweat of their labors was directed toward maintaining the social and economic position of their aristocratic masters. All decisions were made by the landowner or nobleman of the estate. Duties were clearly spelled out; loyalty and hard work were demanded and frugally rewarded. Infractions of the rules were severely punished. In the Western world, this system is formally extinct. Surprisingly, those who share their lives with a narcissist revisit many remnants of this now anachronistic life of service.

Meredith, the owner and CEO of a real estate development company that she inherited from her father, recently married James, her fifth husband. Although the company was very profitable before she became CEO, Meredith took credit for its success as if it had been her invention. James was handsome and debonair. In the beginning, he was flattered by the attention of such an accomplished woman. James was a gifted artist, but because of laziness and lack of ambition, he had never fulfilled his promise. In the early years of their marriage, he was willing to be the errand boy—to do anything that would please Meredith. He overlooked her legendary temperamental outbursts, paranoid accusations, and unreasonable demands. Meredith controlled every detail and decision of their public and private lives. Not the slightest move could be made without her approval. When James followed her instructions to the letter and a mistake was made by someone else, he was blamed and upbraided in front of others. He bowed to these degradations for many years until he became so furious that he could barely tolerate being in Meredith's presence. James perpetually made plans to leave her, but each time his old terror of providing for himself and living on his own overwhelmed him. He hated this weakness but felt trapped and impotent. As time passed and the emotional fatigue of tolerating his life with Meredith wore him down; his role shifted from adoring, selfless servant to intimate enemy.

There is a psychological term called identification with the aggressor that refers to a syndrome that many kidnap victims and prisoners experience. Put in a life-or-death situation, realizing that he may be killed at any time, the victim begins to react favorably toward his kidnappers. In the shock of being kidnapped, he has lost his own identity and fused with the transgressor to save himself, internalizing his beliefs and values. Those who throw their fortunes in with the narcissist are often emotionally engulfed by him and have identified with *their* aggressor.

Intimates of a narcissist are trapped in the role of obedient child. They are not sufficiently grown up to experience themselves as separate, competent human beings, responsible for their own lives. They are uncomfortable activating their individuality, afraid of being assertive, of taking the initiative. In exchange for "security" (often economic), they surrender the intrinsic right to think and do and feel what is appropriate for them. Like a child who lives in fear of mother's wrath over disobeying the rules, faithful servants of the narcissist continually monitor their behavior and follow the prescribed program. They delude themselves that they are protected and cared for like servants of the Old World. Psychologically, they remain children who will never grow up as long as they stay locked in this symbiotic relationship. The narcissist creates special roles for his intimates so they will better serve him. His wife plays the sophisticated, beautiful entrepreneur; the stunning philanthropist socialite; the adoring, decorous mother of his children. The narcissist is writer, director, producer, and casting director of his drama. All the parts are indelibly written and expected to be acted true to the unchangeable script. *No one in this production is left untouched to ad-lib, to be joyfully spontaneous, to play his natural self.*

## FEELING HELPLESS AND ENRAGED

The narcissist believes that only he is capable of an original thought. He shamelessly makes the creative concepts of others his own. Even a written "airtight" contract will not stop a narcissist from coopting the products of others.

Colin, a high-tech wizard, always thought of himself as a writer, despite his lack of imagination and written language skills. He dated Lorraine, a psychologist, for six months. During that time Colin became intrigued by her fully developed concept for a provocative book on office relationships between men and women. Colin listened attentively to Lorraine, taking notes on the subject as a way of showing interest in her. He became disenchanted with Lorraine. He now found her to be physically plain and predictably boring. A short time after the couple parted company, Colin, with the assistance of a talented collaborator, submitted Lorraine's book concept to a literary agent as his own work. The book proposal was quickly accepted by an editor. Colin was delighted, taking full credit for having his first book published. He had long "forgotten" all the conversations he had ever had with his former girlfriend. Several years later, when Lorraine accidentally discovered that Colin had stolen her book concept, she had neither the money nor the energy to fight him. She felt psychologically violated and helpless to defend herself. She had trusted Colin with herself and her creative ideas. In return she had been maliciously double-crossed. Many months after this disclosure Lorraine was consumed by a gnawing rage.

## CHILDHOOD ORIGINS OF
## A LIFE IN THE SHADOWS

The future partner of the narcissist was often the child of an arrogant, demanding, narcissistic parent. From his earliest days he was conditioned to respond to his parent's arbitrary rules and whims. The narcissistic mother or father conducted himself as a dictator, without a conscience, immune to any outside authority. From the time they are very little, these children become experts at catering to the idiosyncratic needs of the narcissistic parent.

In other instances, those who end up in the shadows are raised by neglectful emotionally absent parents. When children have been treated without affection and care, they are incapable of creating intimate attachments. Beneath the psychological wounding lie feelings of helplessness, depression, and rage. These negative emotions are buried because the psychological pain that they wreak is unbearable. They are "forgotten," left in the cold storage of the unconscious. Often the child who has felt unloved desperately seeks satisfaction by turning to a person who promises to satisfy his needs for attention and validation.

Those who cast themselves in shadow are psychologically hungry. Many of them attempt to satiate their appetites through obsessive searches for material possessions. They shop and collect compulsively to gratify an inner void that cannot be filled. Shopping is a food with limited sustenance. When we are on the hunt for "something we must have," the adrenaline is pumping; we are aroused by the anticipation of discovering a "find," a deal. After we have the item or bagfuls of booty in our possession for a while, the thrill and the glitter are muted. Soon we return to our quest for the "next new best thing." The narcissist presents himself as a compelling prize, temptingly served with his promises that we will share his larger-than-life world. His grandiosity and supreme self-confidence fuel the follower's childhood yearnings to finally feel valued.

Joanna could not remember much about her life before the age of ten. She had no memory of her biological father but recounted the comings and goings of a series of men in their modest household. Three of these were stepfathers, and the rest were her mother Sydney's numerous boyfriends. Sydney was consumed by life dramas that involved her latest male conquest. Joanna spoke casually; "Mama was always falling in love." Sydney predictably lived through a series of "love" cycles: hunting for a man, falling in love, the honeymoon period, the settling in and making plans sequence, the inevitable stormy breakup, and then the ugly abandonment finale. Sydney's preoccupation with her "I've got to have a man" episodes siphoned time and attention from her daughter. Joanna was left alone, to fend for herself.

By mid-adolescence Joanna was dating men in their late twenties. At eighteen, while working part-time, she met Kyle, the owner of a large department store. Twice divorced, Kyle had four children, whom he ignored and hardly acknowledged as his own. Kyle was slick and cocky. At age forty he led the life of a free-wheeling bachelor. Joanna was immediately attracted to Kyle's rough handsomeness and reckless bad-boy manner. Kyle began to flirt openly with Joanna, and before three months passed the two of them were regularly intimate. The secrecy of the affair made it all the more alluring for her. Joanna became pregnant and used her upcoming mother role to force Kyle to marry her. Kyle had a short attention span in the character and loyalty department. After Joanna gave birth, although she was still physically very pretty, Kyle didn't find her attractive anymore. For two years Joanna tried desperately to hold the marriage together. She couldn't imagine being without Kyle; he was the focus of her life. After many bitter confrontations and attempts at reconciliation, Kyle abandoned Joanna without the least regret. Joanna felt a deep unrelenting hurt; at the same time she mentally plotted revenge. Divorce eventually followed, but Joanna never let go of her contemptuous feelings for Kyle. He was *the enemy*.

## THE HARVEST OF HATRED

The seeds of hatred are planted slowly, in small increments of cruelty, devaluation, and abuse. Their tiny tendrils thrive in an environment of control, humiliation, and blame. In the beginning, the amorous waters flow effortlessly between the narcissist and his chosen one. Narcissists are highly skilled in the arts of seduction and manipulation and single-minded in getting whom and what they want. It is difficult if not impossible to say no to someone who is so talented at the chase. The narcissist will pursue someone relentlessly only to discover that they won't satisfy his desires. Acting without sensitivity or conscience, the narcissist reflexively drops the person he has hunted so passionately and moves on to the next victim. The course of the harvest of hatred often follows this pattern: idolization, sweet possession, drinking deeply from the trough, the final disillusionments.

## IDOLIZATION

The Egyptian pharaoh, a living god, exercised total domination over the life and death of his subjects. Since they were his human possessions, he determined their earthly fates. Pharaoh commanded armies of slaves to build him a pyramid worthy of his godly status. Decades of work under hellish suns, hoisting boulders by hand, they sacrificed their lives on projects that would bring eternal homage to their master. When he died, pharaoh was elaborately mummified to ensure resurrection in the next world. In a final gesture of annihilation, pharaoh's slaves were forced to certain death as the last great stone sealed the magnificent tomb. Like Egyptian pharaohs, narcissists expect to be treated as living gods. Marital partners and mistresses, though externally indulged, will have paid the price of squelching inherent talents, wasting precious time, and blocking their opportunities for an evolving growth as individuals. As blind followers and worshipers, those who remain loyal to the narcissist to the end suffocate in the airless deadly sealed space of *their* pharaoh's tomb.

Casting one's lot with a narcissist means that your life no longer belongs to you. Your mental freedom and psychological space are invaded. All decisions, behaviors, opinions, and beliefs are filtered through his microscopic lens. The narcissist creates an unbroken fusion with his intimates, treating them like the intricately woven fabric of his own personality. They have meaning only as reflections of his perfect self. Allison, aged twenty-four, was attracted to powerful men who wielded influence in the world and earned large sums of money. At twenty-three, she was engaged to Roy, a fifty-seven-year-old thrice-married vascular surgeon. Manipulative and deceptive, Roy, a classic narcissist, was drawn solely to Allison's youthful beauty, her sexual magnetism, and emotional malleability. He was confident of possessing and controlling her. She was mesmerized by Roy's professional success and the excessive adulation that he commanded as a prominent surgeon. Allison was thrilled by Roy's attention; he was the most dynamic and sophisticated man she had ever met. The possession phase is the early season in the relationship. Allison surrendered her will to Roy as smoothly and completely as a surgical patient who feels the welcomed oblivion of the first drops of a narcotic in his vein.

## DRINKING DEEPLY FROM THE TROUGH

Leftover emotional deficits and traumas from childhood arise and are reenacted by those who are possessed by the narcissistic partner. They want someone else to take over for them. They are afraid to accept responsibility for their lives. Those who fall under the spell of the narcissist drink deeply from his trough of assurances and fantasies, hoping to have their earliest and most compelling psychological needs fulfilled. They are desperate for some kind of recognition, even if they do not earn it themselves. Sharing their lives with a strong personality who appears to be in complete command of his life offers them a way of feeling important and distinctive. They have convinced themselves that they will be cared for and protected by a dominant personality; they believe they have found a safe harbor from life's unpredictable storms.

## THE FINAL DISILLUSIONMENTS

Relationships with narcissists always end badly. They often culminate in financial ruin, emotional devastation, physical illness, even death. They can terminate as precipitously as they started or span over many decades. Their length is dependent on how useful you are to the narcissist and how much psychological abuse you can tolerate. In some cases, the partner of a narcissist has become too ill psychologically or physically to withstand the association any longer. The narcissist effortlessly replaces those who are worn and tired with a fresh face, a bright-eyed adoring disciple.

The narcissist as raconteur is an individual at his most expansive self. With the spotlight overhead, he stacks story upon story that feature him as star of the show. As he speaks, each detail is embroidered or fictionalized to heighten the drama and elicit maximum response from his audience. At age sixty-five, George spent most of his time traveling and partying with his wife, Suzanne. Building on the success of his father's construction business, George had accumulated a fortune that had allowed him to be retired comfortably for the last twenty years. Suzanne, his fifth wife, thought she had become inured to all of George's eccentricities. At the beginning, she learned how to look adoringly as he regaled anyone who would listen with his heroic business war stories. After many years Suzanne could no longer cope with his pathological self-centeredness, his outrageous demands, and his cutting reprimands. She wore a steely smile when George went on one of his nonstop "me" monologues, recoiling with nausea as he told the same story for the thousandth time. At this point in her life, Suzanne was finished, completely disillusioned by her marriage. Each night she was determined to leave George. She deeply regretted all the missed opportunities. She had given away too much of herself. As she lay inches from him in the dark, she hated herself for clinging to this selfish, heartless man. In the morning she woke up and wondered if she could ever give up the privileged "identity" she enjoyed. For the time being, she would perform her mission. Deep below the surface, Suzanne seethed and hissed like a tiger about to mount an attack.

# PART FOUR

# Response to the

# Great Performer

# The Rules of Engagement:
# Holding Your Own
# with a Narcissist

*Ego is a slippery fellow, intent on survival at all costs. If we
don't squeeze it, it's glad to just sit there as ruler of our
domain.*

— LAMA SURYA DAS,
*Awakening the Buddha Within*[1]

We have been fellow travelers on the long journey through
the forests and thickets of the inner and outer worlds of
the narcissistic personality. Seated third-row center, we
watched as he entertained and appalled us with his arrogant sure-
footed strutting, his unbounded sense of self-entitlement, his melodramatic seizures of primitive rage, his calculated cruelties. Now that
you recognize and understand the hows and whys of his outrageous
antics and flawed character, it is time to place the rules of engagement with the high-level narcissist firmly and securely in your capable hands.

Begin with an evenhanded appraisal of yourself, the life you were given and the one that you have created. We all go through tough times. Some of us are visited by tragedy, loss, trauma, deprivation, and disappointment more than others. Many individuals appear to sail through life, gliding smoothly, like a graceful bird riding thermals along a sunny shoreline. This external vision of effortlessness frequently displayed by the narcissist is a carefully crafted façade. Like a photographic layout in a slick magazine, it does not accurately reveal the true nature of human experience. When people tell you how wonderful everything is, reserve some skepticism. Their "Look, ma, no hands" or "I never break a sweat" bravado is construed to make you and others feel small and insignificant. Don't let these folks fool you or allow you to feel diminished or defective. Regardless of their shining exteriors, they are fighting a significant level of pain, concealed deep in the psyche or lodged in the body. Pain that goes untreated becomes inflamed and gradually infiltrates the entire system: body, mind, and psyche.

Living and working with a high-level narcissist thrusts us into the midst of a series of psychological battles. In the beginning, during the honeymoon of the relationship, no one would suspect the hand-to-hand combat that will occur in the future. Even a talented and seasoned psychoanalyst, psychiatrist, or psychologist, who has withstood the attacks and exploits of the most challenging patients, knows that when a narcissist walks into his office (an infrequent event), he is in for a rough ride. Therapists describe how their hair was curled or thinned while "treating" a narcissistic patient. If hardened professionals have great difficulty with this character disorder, don't be surprised when you are thrown by them. Although not a case of life and death, a close encounter with a narcissist can mutate into a stressful and perturbing life experience. To put it in a word, these individuals are *impossible*.

The rules of engagement require a variety of skills. They range from those of a highly trained guerrilla fighter, who acts with full force and precision at warp speed, to the most astute, intuitive intelligence operative, capable of analyzing the subtlest psychological cues of human behavior. Every conflict with a narcissist requires a distinctive style of combat: cat-and-mouse acts, cloak-and-dagger scenarios, spy–counterspy games, or symbolic eye-to-eye sweat and blood confrontations. Mastering the rules of engagement requires discipline, concentration, self-control, and perseverance. Like an Olympic ice-skater, one must practice tirelessly and fall willingly thousands of times with the belief that the next effort will hit the mark. Excellence of performance, pit against the high-level narcissist, is not won through grace or luck but by the fundamental roots of one's character: concentration, fearlessness, and unshakable will. At some point, it is up to you to make an informed decision to stay in the battle to win, to consciously lose for a higher purpose, or to walk away. Any one of these choices can be honorable. Remember, from the narcissist's perspective, he always wins (even when he loses). This is his delusion not yours.

Becoming deeply aware of *your* psychological issues, either through private insights or professional intervention, empowers those who deal with narcissistic individuals. Armed with this level of understanding, we learn not to intermingle the narcissist's ego-driven concerns with the psychological scenarios of our life story. This frees those who are involved with a narcissist from shouldering the devaluation and guilt he so readily projects upon them. These projections are sharp, like a well-honed knife. They are designed to cut to the core, leaving their victim psychologically wounded. In the heat of these confrontations, remember to tell yourself: "This is *his* issue; I'm not at fault and will not carry the blame that is being unjustifiably heaped upon me." As the pointed words bruise your eardrums, you might hear the reverberations of dormant parental voices coming to life: "You never do anything right" "How can you be so dumb?" "You're always making mistakes." "What's the matter with you?"

Owning *your own* psychological issues and not taking on *his* represents a major advancement, a great victory for you. It means you remain whole and intact, inoculated from the narcissist's persistent flow of pathological venom.

## STAYING GROUNDED WHEN
## THE EARTH SHAKES

When the narcissist turns ugly, you feel the earth shifting unsteadily beneath your feet. He has become enraged over some small matter; he's about to blow and you fear that your job or your marriage or your friendship is finished. Your life is hanging by the tiniest thread. Suddenly an alarm is sounding throughout your mind and body. You feel shaky and vulnerable; your thoughts scatter to the winds. Your stomach churns; your bowels cry out. You want to hide under a bed, crouch in a corner, or fly away and become invisible. This is the profound effect that the narcissist can have on us if we are unaware of our own internal psychological processes and are ignorant of the inner workings of the narcissistic personality. *You need to know him better than he knows himself. You also must understand and respect yourself so firmly that you remain unshakable throughout his self-indulgent tirades.*

The key to weathering these eruptions of temper and ego is to become and remain psychologically grounded. A grounded individual is secure and calm; he feels solid at his center. He places value on being real rather than on hiding behind a false image. He acknowledges his mistakes and weaknesses. He consistently searches for the truth. As a result, he has a quality of penetrating insight into himself. An individual who is grounded doesn't permit himself to be exploited by others for their purposes. He views each person as a singular creation. He is loath to make discriminations based on income, social class, level of education, external appearance. Whether you live on the streets or own palatial homes, he appreciates each human life. Someone who is securely grounded doesn't coast through life as if it is an amusement ride. He is always working to adapt and grow within the circumstances he is given. He neither blames himself when falsely accused nor denies his mistakes, large or small. In all situations, especially those that are the most difficult, he strives to be honest with himself. When he fails, he forgives himself and renews his efforts to change course. Persevering and steady, he stands firmly on the soil of his authenticity.

A grounded person respects another individual's psychological space. He celebrates the uniqueness and value of every human being. The narcissistic personality is incapable of making a psychological distinction between himself and others. Everyone is part of him and therefore at his disposal. It would never occur to a narcissist that those who work with him are entitled to a private life. As a result, the narcissist treats others as objects who are answerable only to him.

Bruce, a very successful entrepreneur, earned a good living buying and selling companies. Kenneth, the company's vice-president, the one responsible for ironing out all the financial wrinkles and putting out corporate fires, is a perfectionist and workaholic. It is not unusual for Bruce to call Kenneth any time of the day or night to discuss a problem that is nagging him or some "brilliant idea" that has just come into his mind. Kenneth receives calls from Bruce when he is on vacation a continent away. Although Kenneth is disrupted and annoyed by these intrusions on his private life, he feels that he must have an answer for Bruce whenever he demands one. As long as Kenneth is unable to remain grounded, this issue will not be resolved. Bruce, a narcissistic personality, views Kenneth as an extension of himself. He feels entitled to ask questions and receive the right answers immediately.

It is up to Kenneth to change this pattern. He needs to examine himself carefully and ask why he doesn't deserve peace of mind in the middle of the night or during his vacation. Kenneth must clearly state that he requires that specific parameters be set so that his personal life is respected and will remain intact. No business calls will be responded to at three A.M. regardless of their purported urgency. Vacations must be honored as hard-earned essential time off that cannot be interrupted. Kenneth needs to provide Bruce with a specific plan in advance, one that names another member of the executive staff as a substitute for him when he is out of the office. Until Kenneth feels worthy of the free time and relaxation he deserves, Bruce and future narcissistic employers will continue to take full advantage of these vulnerabilities.

The following vignette describes a successful resolution between an aspiring executive and her boss, a classic narcissist. Debra came wrapped in an extraordinarily lovely exterior. Tall, slender, bright with luminous green eyes and a luxurious mane of naturally blond hair, she attracted attention at work and play. Some men called her striking, while they secretly dreamed of bedding her. Debra consciously nurtured this irresistibility. With a degree in clinical psychology, Debra ran a successful private practice for several years. She soon realized that she wanted to make lots of money easily and quickly. It didn't suit her to listen to one patient at a time all day long when she could be charging an entire group for her services. When Debra visited a friend on an extended vacation, she became intrigued with a course on a new spirituality.

She noticed the popularity of the event, the large crowds it was drawing, all the buzz about self-enlightenment. She knew that this was her monetary ticket. She lifted the contents of the seminar almost verbatim from the clinicians, renamed the course, and began an aggressive marketing campaign. Her seminar became so successful that she had to hire assistants.

Debra worked on a new image to suit this shift to the teaching of her revolutionary spirituality. She effected a convincing sense of knowing and intuiting what others thought and felt. She emphasized that attendees would learn to heal themselves if they took her course. Once people were captured in her seductive greedy hands, Debra applied maximum pressure on those who had completed the course to take advanced sessions (for a higher fee), assuring them that this was essential for future spiritual growth.

Debra charged a hefty sum for her two-day seminars. Assistants—her personal administrator, publicist, and marketer—were paid low salaries. And while she was often late in compensating them, she spent large sums of money on her home and cars and frequent vacations, which she labeled spiritual retreats. If a member of her staff became too popular with clients or began to think independently, Debra devised a plan to dismiss the offending party. First, the carefully dropped disparaging remarks appeared. Then she artfully turned the rest of the staff against this member, using verbal intimidation. Finally, the ax fell, much to the shock and humiliation of the unsuspecting victim. Despite the waves of fear and nausea that rumbled through her offices, she always preserved a stable of venerators who were willing to endure her repetitive abusive episodes. Debra led a dual life. On the exterior, she was the prophetess, the esteemed teacher, the person who had invented an invaluable spiritual pathway. Beneath this image, she was cruel, cold, narcissistic, ruthless.

Shelley, a clinical psychologist, attended several of Debra's seminars and was duly impressed. Debra was taken immediately with Shelley's intellectual acumen and communication skills. She was hired on the spot as a seminar presenter. Shelley was a quick study and soon was co-leading seminars with Debra. The honeymoon between the two continued for a few months. Debra worked Shelley very hard, making outrageous demands on her time and mental and emotional energy. At first, Shelley was willing to invest herself heavily for the advancement of her career and the welfare of the company's clients. She contributed her creative ideas to the project, and as she became more outspoken and independent, Debra became resentful and angry. She persuaded members of her charmed circle to spread vicious fictitious tales of Shelley's character defects. Debra motivated her closest followers to ostracize Shelley. One morning Debra appeared before a session that Shelley was scheduled to lead and told her that she was fired. She used a well-worn excuse, claiming that Shelley was stubborn and uncooperative—not a team player. Inquiring clients were simply told that Shelley had made a quick decision to go on an extended sabbatical. The bare reality was Debra's pathological envy of Shelley's creativity and the interpersonal warmth shared between Shelley and the seminar participants.

Shelley was shocked by Debra's behavior. She knew the truth: her clients were benefiting from the groups she was leading. As a top facilitator, she was making substantial sums of money for the company. Debra insisted that in order to keep her job, Shelley would have to spend most of her time advertising and promoting the seminars rather than actually leading them. She felt as if she was being pushed out.

Shelley stood up for herself professionally and personally. In a private meeting, she told Debra directly: "I have earned the role as top seminar facilitator, and I'm asking to be placed back into the position I deserve." Shelley emphasized: "My hard work and dedication have been substantially responsible for the growth and success of these seminars." Internally, Shelley remained psychologically grounded. She asserted: "I want to continue to contribute to the company's expansion and welfare in the role of chief facilitator and seminar leader." Shelley presented herself in a calm positive manner. She described her vision and goals for herself and the company, and appropriately expressed that she deserved and was entitled to the position she held. Debra precipitously fired Shelly.

After a brief period of adjustment and the realization that this decision had been made for her higher good, Shelley wrote a popular spiritual handbook and began leading her own seminars. Her career flourishes; she remains both professionally successful and true to herself.

## PRACTICE RESTRAINT

The discipline of not acting is powerful. We are not compelled to respond instantaneously to everything that happens. The omission of action is not a concept that comes naturally to us. Most Westerners have a consciousness that continually swirls with a myriad of thoughts, feelings, fears, sensations, and desires. In Buddhism this is called the monkey mind. It moves restlessly from place to place, state to state, reacting to every mental, emotional, and behavioral event. One moment we feel sad and regretful, the next we are restless and apprehensive, and in a very short while we are carried aloft in the arms of a compelling fantasy. Like a monkey swinging from tree to tree, the mind moves from thought to thought, busying itself in a frenzy of activity. Most of us are desperate *not* to know what we are really thinking and feeling. We learn to tolerate mental chaos and distraction as we ride the shifting tides of impulse and emotion.

It is vital that the individual who must deal with a narcissist create a habit of spending time each day sitting quietly alone, practicing mental relaxation, creative visualization, or meditation. When meditation is consistent, we gain sufficient insight to observe ourselves more objectively. As stillness and inner peace permeate mind and body, we develop greater skill at knowing how and when to respond. Just as important, we intuitively sense why and how to hold our reaction. This is particularly valuable in dealing with the restless, combative mind of the narcissist. Running relentlessly from one campaign to the next, he is like a butterfly lighting on one blossom after another, extracting nectar from every flower. Unlike this marvelous insect, the narcissist leaves nothing of himself behind. He makes no contribution to the web of life.

No matter how hotly and wildly the narcissist waves his arms and kicks his feet in a classic tantrum, restraint allows you to take breathing space for your own reflection on what is really occurring rather than act out of fear, anger, or some other self-preservational emotion. The narcissist is counting on your overreaction to affirm his control and reinforce his authority. Allow for your private internal response to his provocations. Being calm and aware, you will respond to him with self-assertion and confidence.

## MAINTAIN YOUR MORAL
## AND ETHICAL VALUES

The prominence of narcissistic values today runs parallel to a growing moral relativism. Those who claim they are guided by conscience are intimidated by aggressive individuals whom they both admire and fear. For many, it is easier to go with the momentum of a stronger personality, despite prickles of conscience that arise. Confronting a fully loaded narcissist can feel as if we are pushing a river. Personal ambition for some is the overriding issue that will result in a compromise of moral values. The last temptation put forth by the narcissist, a clever Luciferian plot, beckons. The "deals" that flow from his gravitational pull are irresistible: a healthy slice of company profits, an entrepreneurial fiefdom, impressive titles, generous stock options. We feel an overwhelming urge to say yes. The hell with the consequences. Ultimately, these promises are empty, grossly overstated, or fraudulent. Those who go along with the narcissist's program have agreed to share his delusional world. They have chosen ego over integrity. These "winning at all cost" and "go along to get along" attitudes have become integral threads in Western thinking and behavior.

Today, those with a conscience are frequently chided as naive, backward, overly religious, simple-minded, and unsophisticated. Over thousands of years the world became civilized because the concept of a personal conscience was nurtured. When families were more intact and intergenerational, the sense of right and wrong was passed down to children and reinforced by the neighborhood, town, city, and society. Several decades ago, conscience and good character mattered. Today, with the epidemic of materialism and acquisitiveness, the drive to *get* often overrides the way we arrive at our destination. What counts are *results*, not how we compromise our integrity to reach the mountain, the private island, the crescendos of unending applause. Today, we are pleasantly surprised to meet someone who has an unwavering sense of right and wrong. Conscience is rapidly becoming an endangered species, the exception not the rule.

Since the narcissist suffers from a severe deficit of conscience, his morals and ethics are mobile and adaptive; his rules for living are based strictly on the end game, the bottom line. The question is not whether he will cross legal, ethical, or moral lines but when. Will you become his collusive partner in an intricate dance that meets the letter of the law? Are you willing to be bought off by extravagant offers of money, power, or a potpourri of incentives? There are always true believers who will fall on their swords or march into hell and give up any last scrap of their humanity to continue their psychological and financial fusion with him. The rest of us are clear that we will either honor our moral and ethical values or struggle to fend off the narcissist's smorgasbord of enticements. The ground of the battle lies within us.

For a number of years, Rachel, a real estate broker with a large following, had been working with high-maintenance clients, Lydia and her husband, Keith. Rachel had a listing for Lydia and Keith's $2 million home. The house went into escrow with a well-qualified buyer. Rachel was experienced enough not to mentally spend her share of the $60,000 commission until escrow closed. However, she eagerly anticipated the earnings from such a large transaction. One of the buyer's inspectors discovered a serious structural problem with the house. Lydia and Keith hired several consultants to evaluate the problem. The consultations resulted in two materially different recommendations. There was an inexpensive but ultimately inadequate and temporary solution that would cost the owners $10,000. The second alternative estimate was $50,000 to resolve the structural issue completely and represented the clearly more responsible approach. Lydia and Keith chose the least expensive option. They were leaving, moving on to the next phase of their lives and were unconcerned about the welfare of the next owner. They wanted their price and were determined to get it without any obstacles in their way.

Rachel explained that by law the owners would have to disclose that through their consultants they had been given two choices and that they had decided to have the less expensive work done. Lydia and Keith's reply to Rachel's admonition was: "We don't want to hear about it. We fixed the defect. Don't you dare tell this new buyer about it. It's no one else's business, and none of yours." After many hours of heated discussion, Rachel realized that her longtime clients would not budge on this issue. She stood to lose not only the $60,000 commission from this transaction but any future business from these clients and possible referrals. She explained in a professional manner: "I can no longer represent you in this transaction since this would mean that I would be colluding in an act that is both illegal and unethical." Rachel walked away from the generous commission and her clients knowing that she had maintained her moral, ethical, and legal standards. More significant to her personally, Rachel had kept her integrity intact and her conscience clear.

## MINDFULNESS

Being mindful is the key to successfully engaging the narcissistic personality. Mindfulness is the art of living fully in the present moment. In this state, you are neither regretting the past nor fearing the future. This principle, which is part of the foundation of Buddhist teaching, can be of immeasurable help in dealing with a narcissist. When we are aware without distraction of what is happening right now, we are drawing upon an intrinsic internal power that is always available. Learning to be observant without making judgments or preferences—not running away from what we like, dislike, or fear—centers the mind. This centering generates a consciousness that is still and sure. As the mind quiets, it gathers greater concentration and focus.

Becoming mindful is a slowly evolving process that requires consistent motivation and effort. The first steps begin with an awareness of our unquiet mind: the spilling of thoughts, memories, feelings, senses, and somatic sensations that escalate, eroding our attention from the present moment. We are carried off on winding detours—fantasies, longings, loops of fear and rage. We move back and forth from current problems to the psychological issues of childhood. For most people, this process is subterranean, buried in the mysterious caverns of the unconscious.

Greater awareness brings a sense of comfort to our being. It provides us with a perspective of knowing what is important and what is trivial. A deepening calmness grows. This process creates a more spacious and secure internal world within you. In this relaxed state, you have the edge with a narcissistic personality. While he is busy, manically plotting his latest campaign, the mindful individual stands securely in the moment, unprovoked by the drama du jour. With practice, we can become immune to his efforts at seduction, threat, and manipulation. With deeper self-knowledge and the insights that come with mindfulness, we protect ourselves against the narcissist's destructive moves. We now view him through the finely cut prism of awareness.

Relationships with narcissists stretch our psychological stamina. We can react to them with feelings of constant embattlement, or we can choose to use these interactions to become more steadfast, less emotionally reactive. Encounters of this kind invite us to flex our growing muscles of consciousness. A narcissist becomes a "gift" that presents us with opportunities for becoming more awake.

## THE BOSS AND THE BOARDROOM

The high-level phenomenally successful narcissist is found in most of our boardrooms. He or she is the president, vice-president, treasurer, COO, or CEO of a multinational corporation, the senior partner of a prestigious law firm, the head of a business empire. The classic narcissist travels atop a magical conveyance that takes him everywhere at his command. On the highway, he positions himself in the fast lane, reminding us of those freeway daredevils needling back and forth lane to lane at lightning speed, devouring the road, endangering everyone in his wake.

What is it like to work day after day, year after year, for a classic narcissist? It appears to be glamorous and exciting. We think to ourselves: "Fate has been kind; he has come into my life at the right moment." In the first stages of the arrangement, we believe the narcissist has all the answers. He is brilliant and clever, a kind of renaissance man (or woman). But this is an illusion, like looking through distorted glasses that show us only what we want to see. Ultimately, the narcissist takes those who work for him on a series of wild rides in hostile territories. It can be thrilling and ego-intoxicating. Much of the time it is simply anxiety-provoking, exhausting, and humiliating.

When you work for a narcissist, your life no longer belongs to you. You and he are conjoined—day and night. No matter how many years you have unwaveringly served a narcissist—decades of devotion and grueling work—he will show you the door in a microsecond. With a narcissist, there are no true relationships. The years of association, comaraderie, and manically fueled dreams fade to black. The sharing of personal histories, old war stories, or tightly held secrets over a martini or two dissolves like sugar cubes in a pot of boiling water.

The narcissist is incapable of either personal or professional loyalty. His life is devoid of true intimacy or love. Every human contact for him is based on utility: getting what he wants, realizing his vision, securing his power position. Like a king overlooking the ramparts of his castle, he covetously surveys his lands, admiring the breadth and depth of his properties and possessions. They are a measure of his feelings of worth and entitlement. As he watches, the king is ever wary of enemy hordes in the forests and thickets beyond. The narcissist plays the role of a paranoid king. Drunk with the wielding of his all-powerful sword, he remains ever alert, eyes and mind shifting in constant readiness for those who would plot his destruction.

A narcissist demands unquestioned loyalty almost to the point of mind control and brainwashing. Ultimately, when you do business for or with a narcissist, independent thinking is forbidden. If you come up with a particularly creative idea or concept, he will preempt it as his own. Narcissists are grabby and greedy. Like a two-year-old protecting his toys against an interloper, narcissists don't share. When someone is loyal to a person who treats him with deceit and exploitation, he has given himself away, piece by piece.

The narcissist is not inclined to go the distance in any relationship—spousal, romantic, professional. The narcissist is fickle but selective in his choice of business partners and associates. A perpetual schemer, he conceives elaborate plans that will lead him directly to his target. His eyes focus on the worldly grail, the golden goblet that will lead him to ultimate power. Those who stand in his way are quickly dispatched to professional oblivion. Like the forces of nature—hurricanes, tornadoes, tsunamis—he appears to be unstoppable.

Those who are hypnotized enough to follow a narcissist can be assured that their experience will run the gamut from adoration to fear to rage to abandonment. It is very rare for anyone who has worked closely with one of these individuals to exit without a mark, a scar, or a mortal blow. Their negative influence is profound. It can cause a variety of effects, including acute and chronic physical illness, psychosomatic ailments, emotional crises, multiple stress reactions, familial upheavals. One would never guess when entering the portals of the relationship that such dangerous and ominous consequences await the unsuspecting victim. This predictable pattern is what I describe as the "love 'em and leave 'em" cycle.

The narcissist begins the "relationship" with the *seduction*. He turns his attentions on you with an exquisite brand of personal magnetism. He's done his homework; he knows all about you. He invites you into his office for a private talk and presents you with an arrangement that will fatten your wallet, enhance your stock portfolio, and fulfill your desires for financial freedom. Suddenly, you feel light-headed and dizzy, drunk with being wanted by someone who is so important. In the first blush of the "union," you are wooed. It is very difficult for most people not to be captivated by the courting of a high-level narcissist. At this stage, charm is oozing from all of his pores like a perfume that lingers on the body of a beautiful woman. The narcissist is appealing to our ego needs and desires—our deepest longings to feel unique, talented, loved, attractive, bright. He is the perfect wave a devoted surfer has always waited for—luminescent blue, building to magnificent height, gracefully shaped, dangerous, an unequaled force—promising the ride of a lifetime. When we are seduced by a narcissist, we view a seamless mask that tells us we are splendid—that we too can become gods. In this first stage, we are not prepared for the merciless pull of the undertow that awaits beneath the wave.

In the next phase, the narcissist *idealizes* his chosen one, experiencing him as all good, a lost puzzle piece that makes him feel complete. The narcissist gets under our skin; he cannot be ignored. He paints a verbal picture for you of just how you will fit in to his future plans. It is true that narcissists choose talented people to make *themselves* look good. You have been picked above all others to share center stage with this extraordinary person. Most people are entranced with the idealization. It soothes and inflates the ego. It provides a tonic to those who feel unworthy and inadequate. It appeals to perfectionists who have never developed a healthy sense of self-entitlement and personal value. For a fleeting time, the idealization provides a salve to childhood defects that whisper "You're not good enough, bright enough, or strong enough to succeed at the highest level."

The next step is the big proposal, the *deal with the devil.* The narcissist offers power, wealth, and prestige to those who join his magic circle. In exchange, he will wield total control over their lives. When the deal is sealed, the unsuspecting one is so mesmerized that he believes the elaborate promises. The narcissist is clever at reading his prospect so carefully that he knows what it will take to make him bite. Like a master fly fisherman, the narcissist understands just what size, color, and shape of lure to use to hook the highly prized fish. The deal is always too good to be true; it will never be delivered. At this point, the unsuspecting person has entered the narcissist's delusional world.

Eventually, every relationship with a narcissist must come to an end. The *devaluation* begins when he decides you are no longer of value. Perhaps he has found a more attractive, compliant replacement. After all, for him, everyone is expendable. This cruel process can take weeks, months, years, or decades. One way or another the moment will arrive. The cues can be as subtle as a weightless feather falling unheard to the ground. The narcissist picks away at the perfect union he has created. You are suddenly accused of making more mistakes. Your missteps are costing the company money. You are derided for alienating or driving away clients. Any excuse that rides on the winds of the fertile narcissistic imagination will do. This is designed to erode your confidence and to justify getting rid of you. In the course of the devaluation, the narcissist uses dirty tactics that include lying, shaming, ostracism, and innuendo. He summons a chorus of willing accomplices who will turn against you on command. In the final stages, you are perceived as a bad influence, an impediment to progress, an albatross that must be removed. Once the narcissist decides to discard you, there are no second thoughts.

*Dismissal* arrives as surely as thunder follows lightning. Often the narcissist uses one of his henchmen to deliver the final blow. By this time, you are not even an imprint on his mind. He has moved on to his next glorious quest. The real reasons for the dismissal are not offered. Like a speck of swirling dust, the memory of you as a unique individual and the positive magnitude of your good deeds dissolve in the atmosphere as if they never existed.

Those who succumb to the *"love 'em and leave 'em" cycle* have been double-crossed by the narcissist and have betrayed themselves at the same time. It is a great disappointment to lose a battle to a narcissist. A graver misfortune is to fail ourselves. Individuals who have traveled the distance in tandem with a narcissist have at least witnessed or been party to numerous immoral, unethical, even illegal acts throughout the course of the journey. If you possess a finely tuned conscience, you will carry with you deserved guilt for those unsavory acts in which you assisted the narcissist. In some cases, the narcissist will leave you holding the bag for the irregular deeds he has committed. Cornered and about to be exposed, he blames everything on you.

## OUTFOXING THE FOX

The fox is a magnificent animal who stalks and captures his prey by instinct. He catapults himself into the air, rising on all four feet, executing a one-pounce kill. Almost no man-made barricade can keep him from ravaging the chicken house if he is adamant. He will lie brazenly on the floor, gobbling up freshly laid eggs. The narcissist is a being who possesses many characteristics of the fox. His actions, like those of a fox, are part of the natural force of self-preservation. The narcissist's aggressive and ruthless behavior is learned very early and forms the inner core of his personality structure.

As long as they don't get caught in his jaws, or act without conscience or compassion, observing how a narcissist activates his gifts of persuasion, magnetism, and self-assurance can provide those who work for him with a cache of information about maneuvering in the world.

Lauren, a gifted independent film producer, climbed the professional entertainment peaks, starting from the bottom. She began as a gofer, laboring her way through many years of twenty-hour days in various roles. She wrestled on the mat with numerous classic narcissists, men and women who wield incalculable power, never hesitating to push colleagues and workers beyond their physical and emotional limits. Lauren spent these years sharpening her intuitive skills for reading people, learning how to communicate and defend her position with controlled professionalism, regardless of the verbal assaults frequently thrust at her. From script supervisor to associate producer, Lauren quickly developed relationships with a few select, trusted individuals who protected her flanks if her growing power position was threatened.

Throughout the years, Lauren was surrounded by many ravenous foxes, sporting for a kill. She dealt with the severe pathologies of classic narcissistic personalities, who were never wrong, constantly blamed others, and obsessively plotted the professional ruin of a driven rival. At budget meetings, Lauren faced down superiors who questioned her judgment rather than taking responsibility for their obvious mistakes and shortcomings. Lauren was a superior student; she always had complete command of the facts, including a photographic mental picture of every detail of the projects she administered. Although not a professionally trained therapist, Lauren was astute at analyzing the unconscious motivations and behaviors of her superiors and colleagues. She knew how to stroke egos and when to apply the brakes. Put on the spot, Lauren became an expert at calmly confronting a fulminating narcissist who attempted to blame her for *his* gross errors.

In tense executive meetings, Lauren would first acknowledge that everyone was under extreme pressure. She offered a series of specific alternatives to resolve the budget problems. This avoided the label of blame. However, if she was accused unjustifiably, she spoke up forcefully and convincingly for herself: "I know you are under great stress during this time and understand your situation. I want to resolve this problem and I have presented several approaches for a positive outcome. Let's focus our energies on these alternative solutions. We can all work together to resolve these issues effectively as a team."

In summary, Lauren acknowledged the issue at hand; proposed precise, workable plans of action and presented them with confidence; and emphasized the value of working as a cohesive cooperative group. She set an excellent example as a competent, grounded individual who enhances her power position while outfoxing the narcissists who surround her.

## PERSEVERING IN THE TRENCHES

One of the most powerful tools in dealing with a narcissist either in personal or in business situations is self-knowledge. Understanding ourselves is a lifelong process. In a sense, the narcissist does us a favor by providing innumerable opportunities to achieve personal insights and to develop self-discipline. He quickly identifies and attacks our psychological sore spots. He digs in where it hurts the most. Whether you seek professional treatment because you are suffering from an emotional disorder or you choose to work through self-discovery—meditation, seminars, retreats, progressive relaxation, bodywork, and so on—all of these modalities will serve you well when you tussle with a classic narcissist.

Begin by studying your opponent thoroughly. Reading this book will assist you in comprehending and appreciating how the classic narcissist operates: his unique character traits, childhood origins of his psychopathology, core conflicts, hidden longings, operatic rages, his sadistic plans of attack.

State the issue succinctly. Do not get personal and vindictive. Defend yourself verbally when attacked by toxic projections. Learn to disagree with clarity and even-mindedness. Be specific with details, not personal feelings, when expressing your point of view. For example: "I understand and can appreciate what you are saying." "This is how I view it." "We can agree respectfully to disagree." Although most narcissists are incapable of self-deprecation, wisps of humor can interrupt the flow of their venom and be applied like adding fine herbs to a luscious stew. Remain open and flexible, grounded in your deep personal perspective.

Like a fine athlete readying himself for world-class competition, prepare your body and mind for the inevitable battles. Most of us are unaware of how tense and anxious we are. Some people automatically accept their high levels of stress and agitation. The consistent practice of deep breathing exercises builds up feelings of relaxation and security within the body. When tendrils of anxiety suddenly strike, an individual who is skilled at deep breathing techniques can shift into a relaxation mode. Progressive relaxation can be enhanced by working with a qualified biofeedback specialist. Hatha yoga performed with emphasis on the breath and gentle movement into the various postures facilitates the body's sense of inner peace and stability.

Ultimately, we must ask ourselves how far we will go down the road with the narcissist. Since he doesn't have a soupçon of conscience, we cannot depend on him to ever "do what is right" for its own sake. Those who work closely with narcissists often become their external conscience by reminding them that if they pursue a particular avenue, they will be caught and held accountable legally. The judgment either to stay with the narcissist or to leave is up to each individual.

It is wise to have plans B and C (your escape hatches) clearly in mind when you are working for a narcissist. Prepare by initiating and nourishing professional relationships that will be both supportive and materially helpful if and when you are ejected or squeezed out of your position. Take the offensive by calmly and decisively creating your very own blueprint for a future filled with challenges that will lead to new levels of personal growth.

Ashley and Ty (a classic high-level narcissist) met during their medical residencies. Ashley knew from the first few dates that she was destined to marry Ty. She fell in love with him quickly and deeply. Ashley became a medical researcher; Ty opened a practice as an ophthalmological surgeon. His practice grew quickly. After a few years, he and a couple of partners purchased their own medical building. Ashley enjoyed her research, but after ten years she realized how much she wanted to have children. Ty had always been lukewarm on the subject, but when she became pregnant, he grudgingly went along. Ty had assumed that Ashley would provide all the direct care for the child or that they would hire a nanny. As soon as she gave birth, Ty became sexually disinterested in his wife. He felt jealous of the time she spent with the baby, although his medical practice was the central focus of his life. Ty was emotionally detached from his son, Shawn; he went through the motions of being a father. After her child was three months old, Ashley hired a nanny and returned to work. But these plans were scrapped with Ashley's profound realization of how precious Shawn was to her and that *her* mothering was essential to his mental and emotional growth and well-being. The thought of returning to her career in the near future faded. She planned to stay at home full-time for the next three years. Ty reacted to his wife's decision with cold rage. He didn't express his feelings directly to her but a palpable tension grew between them. Ty was furious that Ashley would no longer be contributing to the family income. He said to himself: "This bitch is getting a free ride." He couldn't imagine why she would want to stay home with a baby that couldn't even speak. The final blow—she was ruining her career and substantially decreasing her future earning power, thus, eventually diminishing their standard of living. Now their lives were cluttered and fettered by an infant. Ashley convinced herself that Ty would eventually come around and begin to enjoy his son's company. It would take a while—probably when the child could walk and talk. This never happened.

Ty began spending more time at work, coming home late many evenings after his son was in bed. He found excuses to be away from the house on weekends. He lied and said there was a lot of catching up to do, but then spent time with his buddies at bars or in their homes, watching sporting events. He openly flirted with young women in bars and had several one-night stands in quick succession. He blamed it on the booze. Ty rationalized that Ashley no longer cared about him. She was spending all her time with the baby, or she was exhausted. A bumpy marital year later, Ty demanded to know exactly when Ashley would be returning to her medical research. She insisted that she was committed to taking care of Shawn, especially through the critical developmental years from birth to three years of age. Ty exploded. He railed at Ashley, blaming her for every horrible event that had occurred in his life. For a short while, the household was calm. Ashley assumed that a truce was holding, fragile though it might be.

Several months later on a Monday morning Ty went off to work as usual. He didn't call after dinnertime or in the following days. Ashley contacted Ty's office. They said he had been there, but he was always in conference. The police were no help. They didn't want to get involved in domestic disputes. Ashley was hysterical. After a week, she realized that Ty was not coming home. Ashley was in shock. At first, she couldn't believe that this man she had known and trusted for so long and with whom she had a child would abandon her without any warning. Finally, through a mutual friend, she discovered that Ty had found an apartment, was attending work every day, and spending evenings with his buddies. Ashley wept for weeks—moving from feelings of deep abandonment and despair to immobilizing fear.

Abruptly, one day an attorney representing Ty explained that her husband was filing for divorce and that he expected Ashley to be cooperative. She felt as if she was being repeatedly beaten. She developed severe migraine headaches and found it difficult to take care of her infant son. It took all her effort to just get through the day. Estranged from her family, she had no blood relatives to provide support and assistance. While she was able to receive some help from a few friends, they were immersed in their own lives.

Ty pushed the divorce through quickly, negotiating cunningly to pay the least amount of child support. According to the judge, since Ashley had enjoyed a well-paid career in the past, she was not entitled to any alimony. Child-support payments to their son, Shawn, were always paid late, held up for months by frequent disputes. Ashley constantly had to hire lawyers to fight Ty in court for child support. She ultimately decided that it was just not worth it. She would carry this responsibility herself.

She tried to work part-time out of the house, but this proved to be very difficult. Eventually, the house was sold and the equity was split between her and Ty. Because the couple had not saved in the past and had spent a lot of money on luxury items, the proceeds from the sale of their highly mortgaged home were modest at best.

Ashley moved into a small apartment with her son. She realized that she must start working in order to support herself and Shawn. She was hired for a decent salary by a private medical research firm that required long hours and minimal benefits. Because she had taken time off for her pregnancy and the extra year and a half of caring for baby Shawn, Ashley had lost the career momentum she had previously achieved.

Ty never contacted Ashley directly again. His communications took place through the divorce lawyers. She was still in shock two years after his abrupt departure. No matter what the expense to her personally, she was determined to responsibly raise her child.

Ashley spent two years in intense psychotherapy. Working with a skilled therapist, she was able to grieve for the loss of her husband and deal with the disillusionment that accompanied the belief that Ty had never loved her. During the therapy sessions, Ashley recognized why she had been so attracted to such a cold narcissistic man, a charming manipulator, who had fooled her completely. With the benefit of a strong therapeutic alliance, Ashley worked through the critical psychological issues of her childhood that precipitated her fateful spousal choice. On occasions, the emotional pain was unbearable. Ashley wanted to give up, lie down, and sleep forever. But she kept her duties in the forefront of her mind: the physical and emotional welfare of her son and the rebuilding of her life.

For the first time Ashley acknowledged that she had been emotionally neglected because of her mother's chronic clinical depression and her father's sudden flight from the family as a result of his long-standing affair with another woman. As a youngster of eight, Ashley by default became mother and father to her two younger siblings. She put them to bed at night, made sure they were ready for school, heated their frozen-food dinners, kept the home relatively clean. While her mother sank irretrievably into deeper despair and incapacity, Ashley stepped up her duties as the only "adult" figure in the household. There was never any money. Ashley scraped together what they had, bought the cheapest food possible, and grew vegetables to pick up the slack. Sometimes the children had to eat spoiled bread for dinner.

With her strong intellectual endowment and iron will, Ashley excelled at school. She spent most of her childhood watching her mother being transferred in and out of different psychiatric institutions. Eventually, she was placed in permanent conservatorship, and she spent the rest of her days in a psychiatric facility. Ashley had truly been without a mother or father most of her life.

Beneath her strengths and what appeared to be a stiff independence, Ashley wanted someone to take care of her emotionally. With the childhood struggle behind her, she was always worried about finances, terrified that she would one day be out on the street. She was humiliated by the frequent image she saw of herself as a beggar. She longed to marry a strong man who was determined to be financially successful. She had misconstrued Ty's tremendous drive as evidence of character and commitment.

After terminating therapy, Ashley continued to work with her psychological process. Above all, she had learned to be honest with herself. The role she had been forced to play as the strong one who held everyone in the family together was substituted for a part that was much closer to her true nature. She now acknowledged that she could be dependent and vulnerable and express her feelings and even admit that she had emotional needs. Ashley put behind her the bitterness and betrayal of her marriage to Ty. It no longer mattered that she be married to an important man who would take care of her. Ashley felt solid and sure that she could manage her life well.

In her own way and over many years of much internal work, Ashley learned to remain steadfast when she was emotionally shaken by the psychological assaults and mental intrusions of the past and present. She charted her own course. With sails billowing, she now maneuvered her craft through rough and calm seas. Besides pursuing her career in medical research, Ashley counseled women in the difficult process of separation and divorce, supporting their transformation into independent, assertive individuals.

It isn't unusual for us to encounter a narcissist within our own family. It is surprising to realize that one of these impossible people is living in our midst as a blood relative, step relation, or in-law. Some of us have been exposed intimately to full-blown narcissism by one or both of our parents. Dan grew up thinking that his father was the most powerful person on the face of the earth. As a youngster, he worshiped George. George seemed to be able to accomplish whatever motivated him. He was handsome, bright, and dynamic. He also believed that there was nothing he couldn't do perfectly. A classic high-level narcissist, George was driven to win. As a young man, he had excelled at both sports and academics. George was a college golf champion and at one time wanted to turn pro. Instead, he entered the business world and soon enjoyed status and monetary rewards as an inventive entrepreneur. Katrina, his wife of twenty-five years, was the opposite of her overambitious hypercompetitive husband. Psychologically, a borderline personality, Katrina submerged her creative gifts and feelings of self, deferring always to her husband. Although she was kind to her son; she was emotionally remote. Her chief concern above all others was her fear that she would lose her husband if she didn't surrender to his will. In both personal and social interactions, George called the shots. Although Katrina loved her three children, her input was minor in the day-to-day raising of them.

George made the decisions about discipline, schools, their futures. He controlled the entire household, including the checkbook. There were no discussions. He was pasha and king, the ultimate ruler.

Although he had two younger daughters, Gwen and Anne, he ignored them. They were *only* women, who needed enough formal education and social connections to marry well. George's focus was on Dan. He expected his son to become a top professional golfer. George began his son's training at the age of five. He had designed a specific plan for his son's life since Dan was a toddler. He pushed Dan relentlessly. Dan felt overwhelming pressure to bow to his father's demands in exchange for his love. From the beginning, George was very clear that if Dan didn't succeed at college and become a golf champion, he was a failure, no better than a bum. Dan practiced golf diligently and became highly skilled at the game. He performed well academically. In his senior year of high school, he was awarded an athletic scholarship to a prestigious college. His father was thrilled. George believed that he was the one responsible for his son's achievement. After all, he was the chief motivator and trainer. Without him, no one in the entire family would succeed, let alone survive.

Dan went off to college, and for a while he felt that he had made peace with his father. For most of his life, Dan had responded to his father's demands. When he fulfilled George's wishes, Dan sensed that his father was pleased and accepting of him. If he initiated his own plans, Dad came down on him hard. George turned cold toward his son, even hostile. As a classic narcissist, George was incapable of separating himself from his son or the other members of his family. They were all extensions of him. He was the wise man who knew what was best for them, forcing his family into the roles that enhanced *his* grandiose sense of self. It never occurred to

George that each family member—wife and children—had individual identities and distinct needs and gifts.

During the summer after his first year of college, Dan decided that he could no longer maintain the athletic scholarship. He enjoyed the game of golf and was grateful that he played with such skill. He recognized that this pursuit was not his own; it belonged to his father's passionate expectations of him. It was time for him to lead his own life and deal with the consequences. He spoke with George about his decision. George was furious and relentless in insisting that Dan retain the scholarship. There was no compromise between father and son. George made it clear that he was cutting Dan off financially. He raged at Dan, screaming that he had always been a disappointment. He was throwing his life out the window by giving up such an opportunity. Dan was saddened by the venomous nature of his father's response. He took a few of his belongings and went to live temporarily at a friend's apartment.

Cut off financially and emotionally from his father, Dan faced the future with dread. Dan made a decision to initiate a new course. He made arrangements to become a roommate to one of his college friends, got a job working at night for a security company, and returned to school. He obtained a school loan, since he was now financially responsible for himself. Dan decided to become a teacher of learning-disabled students. He changed his major and began pursuing his new goal. Dan had a tough schedule with no leisure time. Sometimes he felt like giving up. He finally graduated, a year later than he would have if he had kept to his father's plan. After receiving his teaching credentials, Dan found a position at an excellent school for learning-disabled children. He felt at home there, working with the students, facilitating their educational and psychological progress. Dan knew that he was contributing his gifts for the first time in his life. He kept in touch with all the members of his family except his father. George refused to engage in any form of communication with his son. In an astounding feat of compartmentalization, he came to believe that he didn't have a son.

Despite the sense of loss, Dan grew professionally and personally as a result of discovering his own path. Within a few years, he became the principal of the school and was responsible for creating a number of innovative learning programs. Although he experienced deep sorrow over his father's rejection of his life decisions, he remained at peace. He felt himself growing—thriving. Maybe his father would one day make an approach toward reconciliation. In the meantime, Dan had discovered his own separate identity. He was no longer willing to drown in his father's dreams. He breathed in the air of his independence and his true sense of value.

Being true to ourselves is a key to dealing with the narcissist even when he or she is a parent. If it means the loss of their presence, that sacrifice must be made so that we can call our lives our own.

## KEEPING IT SIMPLE

A person of integrity and insight leads his life with simplicity, seeing things as they really are, without distortion or delusion. When an individual is not deluded by the world and his ego, it is easier to sort out what is vital to his life and what is extraneous. He doesn't need to continually puff himself up, to reflexively talk about his professional, intellectual, or financial accomplishments. He is grateful for these gifts but unattached to them as the sum total of his worth and meaning.

In his interactions with others, the person who embraces simplicity is straightforward. There are no hidden agendas, no psychological ploys, no manipulative histrionics. A person of character does not feign appreciation or friendship to extract what he wants from you. He has discarded the unfortunate habit of compulsive bragging. He is not interested in social-class distinctions determined by heritage, financial worth, or formal education. He is unimpressed by fame, wealth, or power.

It is difficult for most of us to be unaffected by the worldly achievements and possessions of others. We envy them in secret. We observe the smoothness and order of their days, the privileges and deference, the approbations accorded to them. We feel tugs of regret that our lives don't measure up. Many people embrace these delicious attentions as a goal worth striving for. Some of us are able to shake ourselves awake to realize that what we are seeing is simply an elaborate stage set on which are replayed a series of empty recirculating dramas.

In human consciousness there is an external and internal reality. For some people, the major focus is external: how they look, what they wear, the impression they are making, net worth, professional prestige, popularity. These touchstones define their identity. For a few, transparency is the goal. To put it directly: what you see is what you get. These individuals are like the purest waters of an azure lagoon, where a swimmer views the white sandy bottom thirty feet down. They teach us to be less concerned with living by an image driven by self-absorption or a rearview-mirror preoccupation with the opinions of others. They put no finger to the wind to gauge if they are liked, loved, accepted, or hated. While acquaintances and "friends" twist complex lies about them, they stand firm and unafraid. The man who lives with simplicity cannot be thrown off balance. He inspires us to become less distracted and attached to the glitter of the outer world, the realm of the ego.

The individual who practices simplicity uses his gifts fully and willingly gives them back to the world. He does not charge a fee for being kind. His inclinations to alleviate the suffering of others are unique and spontaneous, emanating from a full open heart. The wise man enjoys his success but doesn't view it as an end in itself. He moves through life without the excessive burdens of self-importance and entitlement. Simplicity brings freedom, like a great wind shaking ripe full blossoms off a tree, scattering their tender bouquets on the ground like the train of an elegant wedding dress. The tree is left standing in its pure majesty with the promise that it will fully bloom again.

# CHAPTER TEN

# *Beyond Narcissism*

*Can you coax the mind from wandering and keep to the*
*original oneness . . . ?*
*Can you cleanse your inner vision until you see nothing but*
*the light . . . ?*
*Can you step back from your own mind and thus*
*understand all things . . . ?*

— LAO TZU, *Tao Te Ching*[1]

When I began this book, my emphasis was on the psychological and psychodynamic roots of the high-level narcissist from a clinical point of view. As the process evolved, I was aware of a shift in thought and direction. At first, I sensed quiet murmurings like gentle, ticklish whispers in my ear. As I moved forward, I felt myself being pulled by thoughts and words that became clearer and more forceful. I listened intently and recognized that there are alternative options, other pathways that lead to personal freedom beyond the psychological gyrations, demands, and games of the narcissist's tightly woven net. In this chapter, I offer another perspective, a way to thrive and grow as a unique individual, despite the narcissist. Consider these alternatives; let them murmur in your ear. Allow them to resonate with you in the most personal sense.

Moving in opposition to the narcissist's convoluted act often makes us feel as if we are fish swimming against a mighty current. Each stroke extracts tremendous effort, unless we learn to shift our perspective and view reality through a penetrating lens, a vision beyond narcissism. The metaphor that comes to mind is that of a fine marathon runner. Spare and lean, his skin shining in the sun, he carries only the weight he must to perform his task. His gait is sure and steady as he moves up inclines and down waiting hills. The runner's eyes reveal an uninterrupted concentration on the challenge he faces moment by moment, mile by mile. His mind and body and the road that he travels are one. He is not distracted by the crowd or the other competitors. He cannot be put off his tempo or stride. Even after twenty miles, a great distance-runner glides smoothly across the surface of the earth, each step a tiny masterpiece of conditioning and will, each heartbeat a testament to his resolve. As he passes by, we are awed and moved to gentle tears by the beauty of his courage and grace.

Today, many individuals are running a different kind of marathon, a trek to a land beyond ego satisfactions. They are no longer willing to live solely for themselves. Gazing inward, they tread quietly, like a wayfarer on a moonless night. Through the blackness, in the distance, they see a tiny light flickering. As they move forward, the beam becomes steadier, more radiant. Others have come to share a journey that leads to a loosening of attachments to our self-image and material longings. With an open giving heart, they are keenly aware of the pain of others, and they desire a reconciliation of past familial wounds, the untying of stubborn psychological knots, and a growing inner peace, a healing stillness.

Many human beings are riding a brightly festooned Ferris wheel of repetition, traveling in an endless circle like a dog chasing its tail. Unable to exit, we unconsciously repeat entrenched habits, compulsions, desires, emotional reactions, thought patterns, and psychological dramas that are unresolved and often unrecognized. These conditioned behaviors hold a fierce unrelenting grip on us. In Buddhism this human state is called *samsara* (the Sanskrit word means "perpetual wandering").[2] Wandering through life in a dream state, we have no map, compass, or destination. We stumble through a wilderness of repeated unproductive actions. We move through our lives, looking for comfort, pleasure, and possessions. The predictable cycle of desire—wishing and wanting—creates an endless pattern of misery. Some seek pleasures of the senses—taste, smell, touch, sound, sight. We are convinced that our survival depends on immediate gratification. Once satiated, we are hungrier for more material and sensory pleasure. This does not mean that we should not enjoy our bodies and minds. What is not skillful is seeking these sensory excesses as ends in themselves. Chronic cravings overwhelm our thoughts and feelings. Satiation becomes the goal.

Most people are unaware that they are constantly driven on an incessant search for the fruits of desire. We say to ourselves, "If I owned that car, I could create a new identity. People would judge me differently—as a success rather than a failure." In another mind, the thought dawns: "If I met the right man [or woman], I could escape from this depressing monotonous daily routine. I wouldn't be alone every night, feeling desperate and unwanted."

Another voice chimes in: "If I had a complete makeover, a face-lift, I would look ten years younger and be desirable again. Everything in my life would be changed for the best."

The Buddha told us thousands of years ago that the source of suffering is attachment: to the body, mind, possessions, other human beings; to the senses; to our ideas—to everything. I remember a series of experiences I had while living on an island in the Pacific Northwest. The constant rain, drizzle, and darkness often made the residents grouchy and depressed but created the lush multiple hues of green that startled the eye and imagination. The island was heavily treed and subject to frequent power outages. I regularly walked my dog on a narrow road that faced the lapping Puget Sound waters. Along the way, I passed by homes of varied architectural styles Most of them were slightly weathered and rather modest. Several minutes into the walk I would rejoice as I observed a vacant waterfront lot distinguished by a majestic old cedar that stood at one end of the property. The tree had a powerful living presence with frilly thick boughs that seemed to reach the sky. Surely it was strong and noble enough to become an eagle's nest. I hoped that the vacant property belonged to an owner of one of the adjacent houses. I had come to believe that it was possible that the lot would remain vacant indefinitely. But I was wrong. Within a year there were stirrings of future plans. Pickup trucks and SUVs appeared. A smartly coifed woman in her middle years started to come regularly. Boundaries were staked, some earth moved. Late one afternoon as I approached the lot, I smelled the strong distinctive fragrance of a cedar tree. I was horrified to see a fresh stump of great diameter left where the tree had been. I almost cried out loud. Why, why, why did these people chop down a tree that had stood with such dignity and beauty for many decades. It was at the farthest end of the lot. Each day as I passed by and for many months afterward, I could smell the tree's essence as if its spirit lingered. I felt great sorrow and anger every time I encountered this spot.

As the months went by and late summer finally brought much-needed sunlight, a large custom home was built on the site—lot line to lot line. The owner had spared no expense or elaborate detail. Even the roof was copper-covered. As the project proceeded, I thought the owner would build some version of a post-and-beam structure to harmonize naturally with the Puget Sound setting. Instead, a house was constructed with thousands of square feet, overwhelming its neighbors with purposeful ostentation. Elaborate curlicues and arabesques of imported stone, wood, and copper encrusted the structure, which seemed to me like a woman in a heavily beaded dress, laboring to move beneath its weight, rigidity, and stiffness. The structure symbolized a paean to self. After the house was completed and occupied, I continued my walks along the road. I could still feel the stately tree that had been felled, like a magnificent bull elephant downed with a single evil shot. I was angered and appalled by this woman's act of greed and selfishness.

One night as I lay in bed listening to the wind and watching the shadows of the trees dancing wildly, I realized that this woman, whom I silently detested, didn't really own this house or the land on which it stood. She didn't own the furnishings in her home, her personal possessions, even herself.

None of us *owns* anything, including our lives. As we become more conscious, we understand that the source of inner peace is nonattachment. When we undo the knots of attachment one by one, we set ourselves free to be the way we really are—transparent as a flawless diamond, bottomless as a crater lake.

Intuition is a moment of truth that arrives faster than a brain wave or the sharpest flash of lightning. It is an instantaneous illumination beyond study or thought. There are various ways of knowing—through the five senses, the intellect, instinct, hunches. Intuition has been associated with irrational knowledge in the Western world. Using one's intuition is thought of as a kind of trick, a parlor game, the product of an unstable mind. Intuition is undervalued if not completely overlooked in solving problems and engaging in creative endeavors. Most professional psychotherapists would be chided for admitting that they frequently used their intuitive skills to diagnose and treat patients.

There are individuals who exploit their intuitive gifts to control and intimidate others. This destructive use of knowing is directly connected with the ego. These intuitions are based on character-logical arrogance and a need to psychologically dominate those around them. They inflict a brand of brainwashing on their victims by using intuitive capacities negatively. These individuals are aggressive and predatory, hiding beneath a thin veneer of personal magnetism and pseudo-empathy. Some "spiritual intuitives," classically narcissistic, solicit devotees and sycophants to swell their cache of followers. Delusional admirers provide them with endless narcissistic supplies: inflated personal power, adulation, and monetary compensation.

The overly intellectual person has great difficulty suspending the persistent raindrops of intricate thoughts that race across his mind. He lives within the intricate labyrinth of a heavily layered mind. His head is full of complex interconnections, philosophies, erudite opinions, countless facts. He is a master at thinking and researching rather than feeling and intuiting. I have been astounded by the deep insights of people who have no formal education. The direct truths that they utter are more profound than the written and spoken words of any number of intellectuals.

The expanding and deepening of true intuition requires the suspension of the rational thinking mind and the quieting of the senses. It demands faith, discipline, and persistence. The highest levels of intuition are developed through regular deep meditation. Meditation, when it is practiced fervently and consistently, brings a calmness to the body and mind. It slows thoughts and quiets emotions. We enter a gathering peace. The nurturing of intuition is done one moment at a time. To be brought to a high level, intuition must become a priority in a person's life.

Intuition involves a special kind of "sight" that awakens when the mind is at peace. Like a treasure that has long lain on the ocean floor, intuition bubbles up to the surface of the sea of our consciousness. In his commentary on the *Bhagavad Gita* (Song of the Beloved, or Song of the Lord),[3] the great Indian guru Paramahansa Yogananda offers a poetic statement that sums up this capacity: "In the lake of intuition, free from the waves of thought, the yogi can see the unruffled reflection of the moon of the soul."[4]

## MEDITATION: DIVING DEEP
## INTO STILL WATERS

Meditation has always been a mystery to me, and in many ways its ineffable quality remains. How can someone stop thinking, feeling the senses, fantasizing, daydreaming, desiring? It all seemed so impossible, an activity reserved only for saints and yogis. Often when we attempt to meditate and feel that nothing is happening, we ask ourselves: "Why am I wasting my time sitting here fidgeting and wishing I was doing something else. My thoughts and emotions are running away with me. I can't stop them." A million times our minds wander, and a million times we gently bring ourselves back to the breath or the mantra that we have learned. We make the effort and continue in the process. We don't give up. There is no such thing as a bad meditation. Devoted meditators of many decades say it is better to meditate daily for a few minutes than to sit once a week for an hour.

Meditation is a highly personal experience. There are so many books and teachers on the subject that it can be confusing and discouraging. Meditation is *not* the absence of thought. It is a process. Each meditation is unique. Making the effort to sit is a triumph. A very wise nun told me to first of all "make it pleasant." Each person understands what that means to him. Experiment with this concept, and discover what you can do to create an environment that welcomes you to go inside.

Find a place in your home that is dedicated to meditation. (Some meditators prefer to perform their practice outdoors. The Buddha often meditated under a tree or beside a river.) By setting up a special spot, you will be inclined to condition yourself to practice there. Make sure that it is quiet and that you will not be distracted by phones, radios, TVs, humans, or animals. Some meditators set up a shrine, where they place special pictures, statues, flowers, stones. A lighted scented candle is a simple but powerful reminder to focus your attention. Appreciating the candle's fragrance reinforces the meditation process. Universal masters like the Buddha, Jesus, great yogis, and lamas remind us that they too were human beings, living in the body at one time, who reached enlightenment. As we gaze at them inwardly or at their images on an altar or wall, we take heart that we are not alone. They are supreme examples of perseverance, faith, discipline, and compassion. They constantly remind us not to give up, to remain steady, open, and optimistic.

Make an effort to sit in meditation before you leave home in the morning. I know this task can seem daunting, but give it a try. It's worth it. The length of the meditation is not significant. Getting the meditation in is more crucial than the time you spend. If you wait through the morning and afternoon, you can find yourself, at the end of the day or at night, tired and unwilling to make the effort, feeling guilty, or simply forgetting about it all together.

There are a number of ways to sit. Some meditators use round cushions designed for practice, which are comfortable for the coccyx and very effective in keeping the back straight. This allows the energy centers in the spine to flow smoothly. Experiment with the feel of your seat on the cushion. Cross your legs in easy pose (lower legs crossed with knees bent), or if you are particularly supple, use half-lotus or full-lotus pose. If possible, meditate in bare feet. If your feet are covered, the cosmic energy may not be as free to flow through the soles of your feet and circulate throughout your body. I find that placing my hands on my thighs, palms up or down, creates steady balance. You can also put your hands, palms up, at the juncture between the trunk of the body and the upper thighs. You may need a relatively flat cushion under your legs. Do what is necessary for *your* body. Experiment with different supports and hand positions until you find what works for you. Some meditators sit on chairs. If you choose this way, be sure you select a chair that is designed to keep the back straight. You may need to place some small blankets or towels under your feet so that you make firm contact with the floor or ground. This posture promotes a sense of security and solidity.

Close your eyes and direct your inner gaze to the point between the eyebrows, called the spiritual eye or the third eye. It is through the spiritual eye, the seat of wisdom and divine intuition, that the meditator experiences the cosmic flow. By focusing his gaze on the spiritual eye, the meditator can direct his concentration to a one-point focus rather than having it dissipate and disperse. This eye position avoids a downward motion that causes distractions and sleepiness.

With practice, putting one's attention here becomes a restorative resting place. Closed eyes promote a quieting of the mind and body. You might find yourself nodding off as a result of sleep deprivation, feeling relaxed, or as a way of escaping meditation. When you are aware that you have detoured, bring yourself back to the point between your eyebrows. Allow your tongue to rest lightly on the roof of your mouth behind the front teeth.

In the West we think of breathing in a literal way. If you are breathing, you are alive; if you are not breathing, your life is threatened or you are dead. We are aware of obstructed breathing because of illness or a chronic medical condition or accident. This is usually the extent of our knowledge and appreciation of the breath. In Eastern practices for thousands of years, the breath has been studied and used as a tool for attaining physical, mental, and psychological health and reaching higher levels of spiritual consciousness.

*Prana*—in Sanskrit means "vital force,"[5]—that animates all of creation. It pulses through the galaxies, deep space, all light, color, sound, every being. It swirls in the cosmos and vibrates in the tiniest atomic particle in our bodies. Prana brings us to life, sustains us, and with our last expiration is absorbed back into the universal cosmic breath. When prana moves smoothly through us, we are in a state of peace. When prana is blocked, we experience disease:

physical illness, anxiety, depression, confusion. Breathing through the nose conserves prana in the body. Breathing through the mouth disperses prana outside the body, decreasing immunity, physical and psychic energy, and concentration. Spiritually, prana is the golden cord that unites the soul with the body.

*Pranayama*, another Sanskrit word, means "expansion of the vital force."[6] It involves many different kinds of breathing that are particularly beneficial to the body and mind. It is important to breathe through the nose not the mouth when doing pranayama and meditation. The nose is designed to trap the smallest dust particles, tiny insects, and pathogens that can cause infection and disease. Breathing through the mouth prevents this protection. Yogis believe that breathing through the nose captures more prana, the power that keeps the organs and nervous system healthy.

Practicing a few cleansing breaths before meditation both invigorates and quiets soma and psyche. As you become comfortable with this process, you can experiment with different breath counts and discover what works for you. Eventually, the exhalation will lengthen. Inhalation is essential to life, but exhalation is the key to the building up of prana. When you exhale, stale air is expelled from your lungs, preparing the body to receive healing energy through the upcoming inhalation. Throughout this process, make sure you are at ease, never forcing or straining. After this sequence, allow your breathing to resume its natural rhythm.

Pranayama soothes all the organs and nerves in the body. It is particularly healing to the sympathetic nervous system, that part of the central nervous system that signals danger: the fight-or-flight syndrome. With regular practice, pranayama restores balance to the sympathetic nervous system, leading to feelings of peace and well-being.

Let's begin the meditation. It takes a while for the breath to become rhythmic and steady. Notice the in and out breath as it moves through your nostrils. Focus your attention on the third eye. Each breath varies in quality. A breath can be halting, coarse, forced, racing, shallow, deep, uneven, fine. During meditation, be aware of the cool air coming through at the tip of your nostrils; on the out breath, notice the warm air exiting your nostrils. Watch your breath move, drawn in and out like the ocean tide. Each breath is a singular event that will never be repeated in the same way again.

Be as unjudgmental and open as you can. This is easy to say but difficult to do. Thoughts, feelings, internal and external body sensations, will come to distract you. Dreams, fantasies, nightmares, obsessions, childhood traumas, and reminiscences will demand your attention. Acknowledge them and gently return without judgment to observation of the breath. Don't watch the clock.

Many experienced meditators offer the advice "Go deep." This means releasing yourself to the spaciousness of a quieting mind. Remain open. Be a joyful innocent in a foreign land. When you are finished with your formal meditation, sit a little longer to integrate the experience and savor the stillness. Let it permeate you. If you don't feel a calmness in the beginning, know that you have accomplished something great. Persist, with kindness toward yourself.

Chanting frees up the constrictions of thoughts that bind us to the cerebral mind. Raising our voices in chants carries us in a different direction on a sweeter wind. Chants vibrate in the head, throat, heart, and diaphragm, creating new possibilities. Chanting, we ask the spirit within us to take part in our practice. We invite the soul to make itself seen and known. The repetitive chanting of the Sanskrit word *Aum* (pronounced "om"), meaning "cosmic vibration," the sound of the universe, loosens and slows cascading obsessive thoughts, errant fantasies, disruptive feelings, bodily discomforts. The "*Aum* of the Vedas became the sacred word *Hum* of the Tibetans, *Amin* of the Moslems, and *Amen* of the Egyptians, Greeks, Romans, Jews, and Christians."[7] Aum is the beginning without end, the continuous force that resonates in every corner and crevice of creation.

Depending on your spiritual perspective, you may discover that using a language like Latin, Greek, or Sanskrit can deepen your devotion. Some meditators find comfort intoning *Kyrie Eleison* (Lord have mercy). This ancient Greek supplication has been spoken and sung for many centuries as part of the Roman Catholic mass. There are soaring Sanskrit chants that calm the mind and awaken the heart. Some individuals find joy and a release from obsessive thoughts and negative emotions by intoning their own personal chants.

Don't pay attention to how long or how deeply other people meditate. What matters is your process. Never feel inferior or inadequate because someone else is a "bliss bunny" and can automatically go into expanded states of consciousness at will. The crucial point is that *you* are making the effort to practice, even for a minute or half a minute.

Gradually, meditation becomes a habit, an integral part of your daily routine. Some people take to it like natural swimmers, baby ducklings paddling silently across a silky pond. They move smoothly into deep waters without trepidation. These individuals are the exception. Many of us feel in the beginning as if we are pushing an enormous boulder up a steep hill. Each day we return to the rock, place our hands there, and don't feel the slightest movement. Sometimes there appears to be no progress whatsoever. But the rock is moving imperceptibly. When we scream "failure," the ego is speaking. Making the effort to sit is an accomplishment. If you miss a day, don't fall into self-recrimination. At the end of each session, take a few moments to meditate for those in need: physically, mentally, psychologically, spiritually. This activates healing in them and you. Subtly, you notice that if you skip a meditation, you are aware that something vital is missing. In your own time, you will look forward to the space that you have created for meditation. It will become an anchoring force in your spiritual journey.

Meditating with others provides extra encouragement to continue the practice. The energies in the group help to sustain concentration and focus. Joining longtime meditators, we feel ourselves swimming downstream against the tide of distraction. We are swept along in the synergy of our multiple endeavors, labors that become a singular attunement to the infinite.

## FACING "BIG D"

Our narcissistic society is strongly fueled by the denial and gnashing of teeth associated with death. Death, the last taboo in Western culture, is a core focus of attention in Eastern spiritual practices in Tibet, India, Indonesia, Thailand, and elsewhere. People in these societies place death in the forefront of their minds throughout their lives, not out of morbid fascination but as a way of freeing themselves to live in the present. The Buddha spoke of using death to learn the most profound life lessons: "Just as the elephant's footprint is the biggest footprint on the jungle floor, death is the greatest teacher. . . . Yama Raja—the Lord of Death—is my teacher. Death drove me to seek the deathless, to seek liberation from the bonds of birth and death."[8] Here, the Buddha is speaking of the freedom from reincarnation, the cycle of birth, death, and rebirth, in which the soul is continually embodied until it is totally purified. Even if one does not believe in reincarnation, the regular contemplation of death is an invaluable practice. It desensitizes us from our conditioned image of its horror. With repeated contemplation, death becomes familiar, more of an acquaintance and less the ultimate bogeyman under the bed.

Death is a reminder that our days and hours on earth must be used to the fullest. By this, I don't mean that we must rush through life—grabbing everything within our grasp. Death is a tremendous motivator to put ourselves in order on every level: physically, psychologically, and spiritually.

When we are caught up in the frenzied world drama that is running away with us, such as a situation at work that has become nasty and out of control with shrill histrionics, or a personal trap that engulfs us emotionally, it is beneficial to regularly give yourself what I call the Deathbed Test. It is the act of imagining yourself at a point near death, reviewing your life and asking yourself honestly what has and does matter at this moment through the lens of your entire existence. Will it add up to the amount of money that we accumulated in property, cash, stocks, trusts, gold, or mutual funds? Will it be that we took an inordinate amount of time and money to look ten or even twenty years younger as a result of plastic surgery and other cosmetic procedures? Will we count up the social and business value of our membership in a particular country club? Will it be the acquisition of fine paintings, magnificent jewelry, or couture clothing and shoes that we accumulated? Will it matter that our child "had" to attend Harvard or life was a failure if he didn't achieve *our* goal? Will we be counting the number of times that we went around the world? Will we cheer that we won a power game over a professional colleague or enemy? Will we care that we had been cheated out of a large sum of money by a sociopath we had once trusted? Will all the human betrayals that we have endured matter?

What will and does survive are the essentials. Are we evolving from our insights and mistakes, even from the cruelties and deprivations perpetrated on us by our mothers and fathers? Are we forgiving ourselves for not being perfect? Are we becoming kinder and more compassionate, especially toward those who are temperamentally difficult and at times impossible? Are we more intimate with the gifts of Nature—her endless exquisite designs and bounty? Are we taking regular opportunities to listen to a bird sing his aria each day at our window at dawn and with fading evening light? Do we laugh and celebrate the frog's midnight-to-dawn playful calls? Do we marvel at the spring greening of leaves pregnant with fullness? Do we celebrate the wind on our faces, making fanciful flags of our clothing? Are we transfixed by the unblinking eyes and sheer glory of innocent animals, wild and domestic? Are we bringing comfort to those who have lost everything, even their bodies and minds? Are we kissing and hugging and saying "I love you" to those we hold close and dear?

There are questions for those on a spiritual path: Are we performing consistent practices each day to make contact with God, the cosmic consciousness, a higher power? How sustained are our efforts to alleviate the suffering of others through our words, presence, listening, and actions. Meditation, prayer, and various forms of devotion prepare us during our lifetimes for death. When the swirling thoughts, emotions, and sensations are quieted and we learn to be serene and steadfast, we make contact with our real selves and with what some call cosmic consciousness. The attainment of this state of equanimity, dropped ego identification, and restful trust prepares us for the transition from living in the body to ascending out of the body at death.

Looking death directly in the face forces us to reorder our priorities. Many individuals who encounter life-threatening illnesses or accidents transform their lives as a result of their keen awareness of death. Making peace with death, they are now capable of living fully in the present.

## KARMA: GOOD, BAD, AND INDIFFERENT

We are constantly in the process of re-creating ourselves. Each action begins with a thought, a sensation, an urge. An intention is formed and an action follows. We all know people who seem to get away with everything. They deceive, threaten, exploit, abandon everyone in their lives: family, friends, lovers, business associates. They perpetrate unspeakable cruelties. Their chronic patterns of intimidation and betrayal become a way of life, as natural to them as the oxygen they breathe. They appear to adroitly skip away from any glimmer of reckoning. In truth, we don't get away with anything in this life. We are held accountable for every behavior—great or small. This is karma. For every action, internal or external, there are positive or negative consequences. Lama Surya Das explains: "The law of karma spells out very meticulously that everything has its implications; every thought, word, and deed has an effect. We are responsible; the lever of our own destiny remains in our hands."[9]

We are creating new karma every moment. All of our actions have a meaning and a purpose. Nothing is random or accidental. Every time we think, move, sense, or feel, we have an opportunity to create a different reality. We are born with free will, and we can choose how we will respond to all of our life circumstances. A tai chi master I knew explained to her classes on self-defense that in any given situation, even the most dangerous—pinned down by a menacing opponent and apparently helpless—you can use something to extricate yourself from the danger. There is a thought, a move, a reserve of strength, a nuance of rhythm. "There is always something *you* can do," she emphasized.

Our state of mind, the quality of our awareness, moods, and feelings directly affect current and future personal experience. Have you watched a relative or friend become more self-absorbed, ruthless, and greedy? Often a classic narcissist, he acts without conscience or compassion. His volatility of mind and the actions that result directly impinge on his internal hell and the consequential pain that he inflicts on everyone within reach. This person is multiplying negative karma—cause and effect are operating. He is reaping the whirlwind he has sown.

We all create negative karma because of our lack of awareness or our decisions to act in a way that is irresponsible, negligent, or malevolent. The words of the Buddha speak as clearly now as when they were spoken many centuries ago: "If a king or householder shall die, his wealth, family, friends, and retinue cannot follow him. Wherever we go, wherever we remain, the results of our actions follow us."[10] Even if you don't formally accept the ancient concept of karma, it is reasonable to believe that we must take responsibility for all of our actions and their consequences. Throughout our lives, moment by moment, we are accumulating the effects of positive and negative behaviors.

As we travel the spiritual road, it is essential that we dispense with our ego, piece by piece along the way until there are no crumbs left. When I first encountered this term, it seemed mystifying, even terrifying. Does this mean that I cease to exist? Do I lose myself and my entire identity if I drop my ego? Is dropping the ego a kind of death? In a sense it is . . . a welcome one. It is a relief to no longer carry such a heavy burden, the many masks of self. The Hindu Scriptures say: "When this 'I' shall die, then will I know who am I."[11]

The ego is relentless in its ability to encircle and tighten itself around us like a deadly python. Letting go of the ego is achieved during a lifetime through a series of steps that include discipline, insight, and meditation. When the mind is quiet, even for a split second, we subtly encounter our real selves. As these moments are strung together, like an endless strand of gleaming pearls, we discover the truth about ourselves. The ego voice becomes muted, as if we are turning down the volume on a radio. Using the tools of discipline and will, we become less defensive, ashamed, angry, greedy, restless, frightened. The mind is honing in on a calmness and serenity that it has been longing for since birth. The intelligence behind all the obsessional thoughts reveals itself. In this heightened relaxed state there is no forcing, just an awareness of psychological and spiritual spaciousness.

As the ego recedes, the persona is freed from the imprisonment of false-self images and pretensions. The masks are removed and discarded. The individual experiences a powerful union with all living beings and creation itself. He understands that he is neither more important nor less significant than others. He is part of an unbroken chain of vibrant consciousness.

## BOUNDARIES ARE AN ILLUSION

Nature teaches us that we are all part of a whole. In recent times, the West has become starkly *individualized.* Today, people are separate from one another. The elderly are isolated, as if they had a pox that will kill others instantly on contact. The deformed, birth-damaged, inordinately obese, disfigured, only *appear* to be tolerated. There are many who won't admit even to themselves that they don't want to be around anyone who appears to be defective or imperfect in any way. The "imperfect ones" are a source of embarrassment, victims of subtle scorn and covert discrimination. When we feel uncomfortable or even hostile toward those we view as very different and therefore unacceptable or even repellant, it is often a negative projection of how we feel about ourselves. Unconscious self-loathing reveals itself in every mental and physical act in which we are engaged. Self-hatred is a toxic waste that both destroys its host and poisons the immediate environment. When we are overflowing with self-hatred, it cannot help but spill and spew upon those around us.

Individuals who remain in life's shallow waters always insist that their experiences have a pleasant, smooth quality, an easy flow. They want to "keep it light." They bask in the company of people like themselves, who are attractive, bright, articulate, and successful. Within the swirl of these tight social circles, there is an illusion of creating a separate world, a false reality that clings to surface matters. These narrow vistas can feel safe and at times giddily exclusive. Eventually, they constrict and suffocate our personal growth. This contrived environment is like a stagnant pond, without oxygen or nutrients, and is destined for extinction.

When we observe Nature closely, we are immediately aware of its exquisite beauty and connectedness. All of Nature is interdependent. The resplendent, indomitable hummingbird, weighing between .09 and .14 ounces, which appears to defy the laws of gravity, comes into the garden just at the right seasonal moment, when special bushes attract him with vibrant hues of red, pink, blue, orange, yellow, and lavender. Their names are familiar, nostalgic, musical: foxglove, hollyhock, coral bell, honeysuckle, hibiscus, bougainvillea, columbine, dahlia, delphinium, larkspur, tiger lily, Indian paintbrush.

The hummer knows just when each bush, flower, and tree has begun to bloom. Flapping his wings fifty times a second, with impeccable form he hovers like a miniature helicopter, placing his tapered bill into each delicate blossom. He systematically moves from one flower to the next, penetrating each one, not missing the tiniest bloom. During his voracious feeding, the hummingbird accumulates pollen on his body that causes adjacent flowers to proliferate. Naturalists tell us that there are specific flowers that are designed to allow the hummingbird to thrive. The minuscule light-as-a-feather hummer will, in his lifetime, be responsible for creating profusions of flowers.

The hummingbird is a symbol of Nature overcoming impossible obstacles. These tiny marvels migrate 1,800 miles from the northeastern United States to Central America. They travel 600 miles across the Gulf of Mexico without stopping to rest. The hummingbird inspires all of us with his iridescent beauty and the soaring, unwavering, joyful way he shares his life with us.

In humans, as in all of Nature, there are no boundaries: skin to skin, breath to breath, smile to smile, tear to tear, eye to eye, we are one. We are sky and sea, meeting with seamless beauty. As the sun melts below the horizon, mystical hues rise and fall into one another: tangerine, alizarin crimson, lavender, violet, indigo, midnight blue. Sky and sea rest in each other's arms.

Whatever pathway you take beyond narcissism, it is *your* process. Dogma, rules, prohibitions, intimidations, or authorities cannot tell you which direction or how far or deep you need to travel to reach your true self. The journey has neither beginning nor end. The path can be smooth or rocky, desert or swamp. Winds blow the sands, making it impossible to see; the snow is hip deep; bone-breaking ice awaits your heavy fall. At a sudden clearing, the sky bursts eternal blue, horizon to horizon. For a long moment you see things as they really are, without delusion. There are others who have traveled centuries before you and those who are on their way now. Great teachers, prophets, and holy men like Jesus and Buddha resonate within us through their words and the evidence of their lives.

If you decide to take this journey, tune into your intuition. Persevere no matter how difficult, discouraging, or exasperating it becomes. At way stations you will discover those who are also trekking the path. They will quench your thirst with their kindness and encouragement, offer insights that inspire you to take the next step.

Follow the beam of light that stands before you. In many Eastern spiritual disciplines the invitation beckons to close your eyes, gaze at the point between your eyebrows (the third eye), and surrender to the true reality beneath the chatter, mental gymnastics, emotional uproars, obsessive thoughts, regrets, and hurts you are holding. Allow them to dissolve through an open heart and a will determined to achieve a higher consciousness. Here, the clear light of intuition is the brightest star in your sky. The earth's winds quiet, the senses still, the past is washed clean, the ego fades, an unexpected peace begins to dawn. Now you are home.

> *Feel your soul dance in the eyes of the infant,*
> *Creating new worlds—spinning, sparkling, transcendent.*

# Notes

CHAPTER ONE: *At Center Stage*

1. George Eliot, *Adam Bede*, in *The Macmillan Dictionary of Quotations* (New York: Macmillan, 1989), p. 31.
2. www.aphids.com/cgi-bin/quotes
3. Ariana Huffington, *Pablo Picasso: Creator and Destroyer* (New York: Avon, 1996), p. 48.
4. Françoise Gilot and Carlton Lake, *Life with Picasso* (New York: Anchor, 1989), p. 84.
5. Ibid.
6. Ibid., p. 349.
7. Ibid., p. 142.
8. Ibid., p. 142.
9. Ibid., p. 335.
10. Ibid., p. 355.
11. Marina Picasso, in collaboration with Louis Valentin, *Picasso, My Grandfather* (New York: Riverhead, 2001), p. 5.
12. The Picasso virus refers to the self-destructive effect that Picasso had on all of those close to him—family, wives, friends, and so on. See ibid., p. 31.
13. Huffington, p. 465.
14. *Diagnostic and Statistical Manual of Mental Disorders*, 4th ed., (*DSM-IV-TR*) (Washington, D.C.: American Psychiatric Association, 2000), p. 717.
15. Ibid., p. 701.
16. Ibid., pp. 93–99.
17. Ibid., pp. 701–706.
18. Susan Bridle, "The Seeds of the Self: An Interview with Otto Kernberg" (www.wie.org/j17/kern.asp, p. 1).
19. Rollo May, *The Cry for Myth* (New York: W. W. Norton, 1991), p. 117.
20. Ibid., p. 112.
21. Barry Paris, *Audrey Hepburn* (New York: G. P. Putnam's Sons, 1996), p. 364.

CHAPTER TWO: *The Image Maker*
1. Donald Spoto, *Blue Angel: The Life of Marlene Dietrich* (New York: Doubleday, 1992), p. 302.


CHAPTER THREE: *The Exploiter*
1. William Shakespeare, *King Henry the Sixth, Part III.* http://www.giga-usa.com
2. Christopher Lasch, *The Culture of Narcissism: American Life in an Age of Diminishing Expectations* (New York: Warner, 1979), p. 396.
3. Edward Jay Epstein, *Dossier: The Secret History of Armand Hammer* (New York: Carroll and Graf, 1999), p. 193.
4. Carl Blumay, with Henry Edwards, *The Dark Side of Power: The Real Armand Hammer* (New York: Simon & Schuster, 1992), p. 79.
5. Ibid., p. 442.
6. Ibid., p. 443.
7. Epstein, p. 14.
8. Ibid., p. 297.
9. Ibid., p. 14.
10. Blumay, p. 174.
11. Ibid., p. 175.
12. Epstein, p. 352.
13. Ibid.


CHAPTER FOUR: *Golden Child*
1. Meryle Secrest, *Frank Lloyd Wright: A Biography* (Chicago: University of Chicago Press, 1992), p. 52.
2. Brendan Gill, *Many Masks: A Life of Frank Lloyd Wright* (New York: Da Capo, 1998), p. 34.
3. Ibid., p. 26.
4. Ibid, p. 35.
5. Ibid., p. 27. Taken originally from *Frank Lloyd Wright: An Autobiography*, 2nd ed. (Duell, Sloan and Pearce, 1943), p. 11.
6. Secrest, p. 52.
7. Ibid.
8. Ibid.
9. Ibid.
10. Gill, p. 34.
11. Ibid.
12. Secrest, p. 201.
13. Ibid.
14. Gill, p. 40.

15. D. W. Winnicott, *The Maturational Processes and the Facilitating Environment: Studies in the Theory of Emotional Development* (New York: International Universities Press, 1985), p. 148.
16. Ibid., p. 145.

CHAPTER FIVE: *The Well of Emptiness*
1. Otto Kernberg, *Borderline Conditions and Pathological Narcissism* (New York: Jason Aronson, 1985), p. 220.


CHAPTER SIX: *Hardened Heart*
1. William Shakespeare, *Othello*, IV, i, 190. In John Bartlett, *Familiar Quotations: A Collection of Passages, Phrases and Proverbs Traced to Their Sources in Ancient and Modern Literature*, 15th ed. (Boston: Little, Brown, 1980), p. 231.
2. Erik H. Erikson, *Identity and the Life Cycle* (New York: W. W. Norton, 1980), p. 57.
3. Ibid.
4. Barbara Branden, *The Passion of Ayn Rand* (New York: Anchor, 1986), p. xi.
5. Ibid., p. 7.
6. Chris Matthew Sciabarra, *Ayn Rand: The Russian Radical* (University Park: Pennsylvania State University Press, 1995), p. 66.
7. Barbara Branden, pp. 259–260.
8. Nathaniel Branden, *My Years with Ayn Rand* (San Francisco: Jossey-Bass, 1999), p. 145.
9. Ibid., p. 137.
10. Barbara Branden, p. 271.
11. Ibid., p. 339.
12. Nathaniel Branden, p. 343.


CHAPTER SEVEN: *The Charmed Circle*
1. Gill, p. 446.
2. Ibid., p. 48.
3. Secrest, p. 314.
4. Gill, p. 514.


CHAPTER EIGHT: *The Intimate Enemy*
1. Proverbs 27:5–6. In John Bartlett, *Familiar Quotations: A Collection of Passages, Phrases and Proverbs Traced to Their Sources in Ancient and Modern Literature*, 15th ed. (Boston: Little, Brown, 1980), p. 25.

CHAPTER NINE: *The Rules of Engagement*

1. Lama Surya Das, *Awakening the Buddha Within: Eight Steps to Enlightenment* (New York: Broadway, 1998), p. 394.


CHAPTER TEN: *Beyond Narcissism*

1. Lao Tzu, *Tao Te Ching* (New York: Harper & Row, 1988), p. 10.
2. Lama Surya Das, p. 101.
3. Liza Lowitz and Reema Datta, *Sacred Sanskrit Words for Yoga, Chant, and Meditation* (Berkeley, Calif.: Stone Bridge, 2005), p. 51.
4. Paramahansa Yogananda, *The Bhagavad Gita: Royal Science of God-Realization*, vol. 1. (Los Angeles: International Publications Council of Self-Realization Fellowship, 2001), p. xvii.
5. David Frawley, *Yoga and Ayurveda: Self-Healing and Self-Realization* (Twin Lakes, Wisc.: Lotus, 1999), p. 242.
6. Ibid.
7. Yogananda, pp. 1007–1008.
8. Lama Surya Das, pp. 103–104.
9. Ibid., p. 110.
10. Ibid., p. 129.
11. Yogananda, p. 84.

# References

*Books*

American Psychiatric Association. *Diagnostic and Statistical Manual of Mental Disorders*, 4<sup>th</sup> ed. (DSM-IV-TR). Washington, D.C.: American Psychiatric Association, 2000.

Blumay, Carl, with Henry Edwards. *The Dark Side of Power: The Real Armand Hammer*. New York: Simon & Schuster, 1992.

Branden, Barbara. *The Passion of Ayn Rand*. New York: Anchor, 1986.

Branden, Nathaniel. *My Years with Ayn Rand*. San Francisco: Jossey-Bass, 1999.

Epstein, Edward Jay. *Dossier: The Secret History of Armand Hammer*. New York: Carroll and Graf, 1999.

Erikson, Erik H. *Identity and the Life Cycle*. New York: W. W. Norton, 1980.

Frawley, David. *Yoga and Ayurveda: Self-Healing and Self-Realization*. Twin Lakes, Wisc.: Lotus, 1999.

Gill, Brendan. *Many Masks: A Life of Frank Lloyd Wright*. New York: Da Capo, 1998.

Gilot, Françoise, and Carlton Lake. *Life with Picasso*. New York: Anchor, 1989.

Huffington, Ariana. *Pablo Picasso: Creator and Destroyer*. New York: Avon, 1996.

Kernberg, Otto. *Borderline Conditions and Pathological Narcissism*. New York: Jason Aronson, 1985.

—. *Severe Personality Disorders: Psychotherapeutic Strategies*. New Haven and London: Yale University Press, 1986.

Lao Tzu. *Tao Te Ching*. Translated by Stephen Mitchell. New York: Harper & Row, 1988.

Lasch, Christopher. *The Culture of Narcissism: American Life in an Age of Diminishing Expectations*. New York: Warner, 1979.

Lowitz, Leza, and Reema Datta. *Sacred Sanskrit Words for Yoga, Chant, and Meditation*. Berkeley, Calif.: Stone Bridge, 2005.

May, Rollo. *The Cry for Myth.* New York: W. W. Norton, 1991.

Paris, Barry. *Audrey Hepburn.* New York: G. P. Putnam's Sons, 1996.

Picasso, Marina, in collaboration with Louis Valentin. *Picasso, My Grandfather.* New York: Riverhead, 2001.

Sciabarra, Chris Matthew. *Ayn Rand: The Russian Radical.* University Park: Pennsylvania State University Press, 1995.

Secrest, Meryle. *Frank Lloyd Wright: A Biography.* Chicago: University of Chicago Press, 1992.

Spoto, Donald. *Blue Angel: The Life of Marlene Dietrich.* New York: Doubleday, 1992.

Surya Das, Lama. *Awakening the Buddha Within: Eight Steps to Enlightenment.* New York: Broadway, 1998.

Winnicott, D. W. *The Maturational Processes and the Facilitating Environment: Studies in the Theory of Emotional Development.* New York: International Universities Press, 1985.

Yogananda, Paramahansa. *The Bhagavad Gita: Royal Science of God-Realization,* vols. 1 and 2. Los Angeles: International Publications Council of Self-Realization Fellowship, 2001.


*Online Sources*

Bridle, Susan. "The Seeds of the Self: An Interview with Otto Kernberg." www .wie.org/j17/kern.asp

www.birds-n-garden.com/hummingbirds

www.portalproductions.com/h/behavior

www.themystica.org/mythical-folk/-articles/v/vasudeva

# Index

Abandonment, fear of, 22
Abuse, 158
Achievements, identity based on, 43
Achievers, 12
Acquisitiveness, 100
Actor, consummate, 57
*Adam Bede* (Eliot), 3
Admiration
  need for, 19, 52
  requiring excessive, 19
  of Wright, F. L., 10
Adoring audience, 137–62
Adulation
  in entertainment industry, 101
  Picasso receiving, 18
Aesthetic imperfections, 27
Affective memory, 25
Aggression, 23
Aging
  horror of, 110
  image and, 39–40
  *See also* Youth-enhancing procedures
Alcohol, to escape pain, 129–30
Alone time, 174
Ambition, 175
Amen, 211

*Amin*, 211
Anaesthesia, psychological, 128–29
Anger, 103
Antisocial personality, 6, 22, 23
Aphrodite, 12
Appearance
  of goodness, 33
  partner choice based on, 45
  *See also* Image
Applause, world's, 35–36
Armand Hammer Center for Cancer Biology, 71
Armand Hammer Museum, 70
Arrogance, 20
  of parents, 156
*Atlas Shrugged* (Rand), 118, 121
Attachment, 202–3. *See also* Nonattachment
Attention, of narcissists, 31
Audience. *See* Adoring audience
*Aum* ("om"), 211
*Awakening the Buddha Within* (Surya Das), 165
Awareness, 174
  of end game, 60
  greater, 178
  quality of, 216

Selfishness, 57, 111
  of parents, 94
Senses
  intuition and, 204–5
  pleasures of, 201
Servants, selfless, 152–55
Service, 41
Sexual affairs, 101–2. *See also*
    Mistresses
Shakespeare, William, 51, 113
Shamelessness, 64
Shopping, 157
Simon, Luc, 16
Simplicity, 196–98
Slights. *See* Injuries and slights
Snobbery, 30
Social status, attraction of, 18
Society
  encouraging high-level
      narcissism, 6
  narcissism reinforced by, 26
Soul
  heart opening, 220–21
  losing, 111
Soviet Academy of Arts, 69
Space, psychological, 30–31
Specialness, 19. *See also* Golden child
Spiritual eye, 208, 220
Spiritual intuitives, 204
Spiritual lite, 57–59
Spirituality
  death and, 212–15
  empathy developed through,
      131–34
  narcissism as opposite of, 59
  pseudo-, 58
  questions for path of, 214
  for softening heart, 132
Spiritualization, 59
Spoto, Donald, 37
Spouses, as selfless servants, 152
Stability, 197
Stillness, of mind, 174
Straightforwardness, 197

Studying, of opposition, 186–87
Suffering
  in Buddhism, 202
  conscious, 127–31
  dealing with, 128
  truth transforming, 130
Superiority, 78
Supporting actors, 146–48
Surviving, narcissism, 186–96
Surya Das (Lama), 165
  on karma, 215
Suspicion, 66, 107
Symbiosis, 88, 89, 155

Tai chi, 216
Talent, 45
Taliesin, 81, 84
Taliesin Fellowship, 138, 139, 141
Taliesin North, 138
Taliesin West, 138
*Tao Te Ching* (Lao Tzu), 199
Thinking, suspension of rational, 205
Third eye, 208, 220
Tolman, Francis, 68–69
Transparency, 132
  as goal, 197
Treachery, 72
  of Hammer, 8
  murderous intentions of, 74
True self, 92, 95
Trust, 115
Truthfulness, 26, 27
  appreciating our own, 131
  greatness and, 41–42
  image and, 41–42
  intuition and, 204–5
  suffering transformed by, 130

Unbroken union, 88–91
Underhandedness, 57
Unhealthy narcissism, 12
Union, unbroken, 88–91
United Nation's Children Fund
    (UNICEF), 36

# About the Author

Linda Martinez-Lewi holds a Ph.D. in clinical psychology and is a licensed marriage and family therapist. She lives in Carlsbad, California.

If you enjoyed this book, visit

**www.tarcherbooks.com**

and sign up for Tarcher's e-newsletter to receive
special offers, giveaway promotions, and
information on hot upcoming releases.

TARCHER
PENGUIN

*Great Lives Begin with Great Ideas*

**Connect with the Tarcher Community**

· · ·

Stay in touch with favorite authors
Enter weekly contests
Read exclusive excerpts!
Voice your opinions!

**Follow us**

 Tarcher Books

 @TarcherBooks